To Mollie Lee
with much love
Mother
5/15/92

Mollie Lee Pryor

Mollie Lee
Pryor

Victoria

Moments
IN THE
Garden

Victoria

$\mathcal{M}$OMENTS
IN THE
$\mathcal{G}$ARDEN

Text by Tovah Martin
Photographs by Toshi Otsuki
Foreword by Enid A. Haupt
Introduction by Nancy Lindemeyer

HEARST BOOKS
New York

Martin, Tovah.
   Victoria moments in the garden / text by Tovah Martin ;
photographs by Toshi Otsuki, — 1st U.S. ed.
      p.   cm.
   ISBN 0-688-09736-7
   1. Gardens—United States.   2. Gardens—United States—
Pictorial works.   I. Title.
SB466.U6M29   1991
712'.6'0973—dc20   91-8411
                                                           CIP

Printed in Singapore
First U.S. Edition

1 2 3 4 5 6 7 8 9 10

For *Victoria*—
Nancy Lindemeyer, Editor
Bryan E. McCay, Art Director
John Mack Carter, Director, Magazine Development

Edited by Charles A. de Kay
Designed by Barbara Scott-Goodman

Produced by Smallwood and Stewart, Inc.
New York City

CONTENTS

FOREWORD

OMENTS IN THE GARDEN takes you on a tour of horticultural splendor. The book is a two-fold treasure: Biographically informative text illuminates a collection of marvelous photographs of some of the most romantic public gardens America has to offer. The founders of each garden come alive in text profiles—the descriptions would lead you to believe that the author interviewed each personally. Breathtaking pictures reveal a wide range in the kinds of gardens that might be called romantic; this variety, in many ways, reflecting the individuals who created them.

I have often visited Dumbarton Oaks, for example, and I've been there in every season. But until I read this book I thought they had built the house and gardens simply to suit their superb art collection. The collection is varied, covering many forms of art from a good many countries. The noted ambassador Robert Bliss and his wife Mildred Bliss searched the world for the best examples of art native to where they were posted. As one tours the house and the gardens, one notices each is developed to best display their artistic treasures during different seasons. Reading the chapter, I was delighted to discover the story of the deep friendship between the mistress of the house, Mildred Bliss, and America's foremost female landscape architect, Beatrix Farrand. The tale of the gardens' development is one rooted deeply in the mutual respect and understanding these women shared for each other.

On the other hand, the gardens at Joanna Reed's farm are a reflection of her own singular personality. As a wife and mother of five children, she has created many flower gardens to serve a variety of purposes. On the whole she enjoyed much success. In one certain area, however, she wanted to create an aspect of formality. The climate did not respond favorably to her plantings, and the following year she used a new combination of plant materials. This particular garden has subsequently become her ultimate joy.

Longwood Gardens, outside Philadelphia, are known worldwide. The story of their founding is less well-known. Here we read how the creator, Pierre du Pont, re-created and reworked from memory garden designs which he brought back from his travels. I believe Longwood is easily one of the most superb gardens in the country. The institution has become the center for American gardening, featuring, among its many attributes, a school for students of horticulture which has sent many young professional gardeners into the world. The garden has year-round activities that appeal to gardeners of all levels of expertise and to garden-lovers. In summer, there are many events for day and evening enjoyment. In my visits during the autumn and winter, the greenhouse gardens stand out as being particularly beautiful. They contain the greatest examples of palms, plants, and flowers of all varieties of any I've ever seen. Holiday decorations make a visit to the greenhouses inspirational.

In a romantic vein, readers will love the charming story of Elizabeth and Edwin Clarkson. The Clarksons attracted a great number of birds to their gardens. The name of their estate, Wing Haven, is touchingly poetic. It is not often that we read of bird-

lovers' dedication to their gardens, and this is a special one, created by an especially lovely couple. Because Elizabeth was of frail health, the Clarksons made a ritual of their home life with the birds and their gardens. They built a six-foot brick wall to protect the birds from harm. They planted shrubs and trees to give their feathered friends comfortable places to nest and to make sure that they had plenty to eat. It is nice to know that after a long life, Elizabeth Clarkson's birds remain loyal to her memory. They continue to return to Wing Haven as though she were still there.

The poet Emily Dickinson became a legendary figure through the garden she developed. She dedicated her mature years to the garden, and her poetry reflects the serenity that she found there. Her garden became the inspiration for her verse during the years of her self-induced seclusion from society.

Polls show that in the United States today gardening is the most popular hobby. A burgeoning awareness of the need for conservation is sweeping the country at the same time. This new consciousness of our environment has brought many people to try to preserve nature wherever they can. It is fascinating to discover that the stories of a great many of the enchanting gardens featured in MOMENTS IN THE GARDEN are actually the stories of how they were rescued by loving hands from neglect and disrepair. Concerned neighbors banded together to volunteer their time and energies to restore such national treasures as Cranbrook gardens, Celia Thaxter's garden, and the gardens at the Emily Dickinson Homestead to their former glory.

Enid A. Haupt
Spring, 1991

PREFACE

Certain gardens tarry in your memory. They are the enchanted places where azaleas spill exuberantly down hillsides or blossom-bedecked perennials float hauntingly on evening mists. They have nothing in common with one another except perhaps their ability to cast a spell softly on the present and leave their impression indelibly to color future daydreams.

Certain moments stay with you forever. A rose kissed by fragile morning sunlight, a carpet of wind-strewn camellia flowers freshly fallen, or a bud ripe and ready to burst into petals—those moments are never forgotten.

Over the years I—and all the editors at *Victoria*—have wandered through countless gardens. We have been touched on so many moments. This book is a glimpse at our most precious memories, in its pages we share our favorite gardens in the hope that they will touch and inspire you as well.

The gardens that appear on these pages were selected because they are magical. They are an eclectic array—Emily Dickinson's garden is but a wee plot whereas Longwood spreads its sumptuous botanical feast over more than a thousand acres. Dumbarton Oaks is tucked not far from the bustle of downtown Washington, D.C. while Joanna Reed's Longview Farm is nestled in the heart of the rambling countryside. Cranbrook is carefully clipped, while Garden in the Woods is delightfully wild. Some are over a century old, while others are still evolving. Yet, they all have a common romance. Each garden has a shining, inner beauty that remains intimate while you wander and lingers long after you leave. There is something very personal about these places. All have a quiet peacefulness and yet each takes your breath away.

This is the gentlest of all possible tour books. Throughout its pages we travel through gardens, recounting their history, introducing both their creators and their botanical cast of characters. And yet, this is not an exhaustive guide. We selected our favorite nooks and strolled rapidly past places that

did not spark our imagination.

Together we labored to understand these incredible places and share our understanding. Toshi's task was to distill the soul of a garden onto film and hold it poised in time. He portrayed the roses as the sun illuminated their glowing petals moments after a rainstorm pelted their fertile beds. My job was to reveal the overall drama of the rose garden and describe the surrounding scene. I attempted to recount how that rose came to grow so salubriously in its deep, rich bed despite the mischief of innumerable rainstorms.

Just as snippets from treasured gardens never fade from your memory, we wanted to give you a book that would stay with you always. Not only does this book capture outstanding moments in the garden, it also shares the secrets behind this country's most enchanted landscapes. In its pages, we lead you past fantastic wisteria standards dripping in lavender splendor, and we also share the techniques that might allow you to create similar artistry. We lead you down garden steps and describe how a stairway might be arranged to ease your footfall. We meander through medieval gardens and then introduce appropriate herbs essential to composing a similar scene.

We spread violet beds at your feet and describe how you, too, might cultivate a profusion of fragrant violets. We hope to show you the fantasy of these gardens, but we want also to reveal the problems that gardeners courageously surmount to craft such special places. Gardening, after all, is an art of touching and feeling, shaping and designing. It must be felt firsthand.

Most importantly, we want you to visit these gardens and return home with a pocket full of memories. We are proud that all the landscapes presented in this volume are American gardens. Many have been lovingly preserved to withstand the ravages of time so you might enjoy their pleasures. They spread throughout the countryside from the West Coast to the East, from the South to the upper Midwest. We hope that you will seek them out. We hope that you will plant places of your own that will sprout and blossom with wonderful daydreams. In the meantime, wander through these pages and partake of many delicious moments in the garden.

Tovah Martin
Spring, 1991

At the Bishop's Garden, an isolated bench offers a spot for quiet conversation.

INTRODUCTION

"Many a garden has left its memory with me . . ."

Colette

When I was at college the green velvet lawns of our campus rolled gently down to the city's rose garden, almost as a carpet beckoning me to visit. Even when they were not in full bloom, the orderly rows and pretty arbors set amidst tiny streams with white footbridges provided a haven during my student years. That garden was perhaps the first one to imprint on my heart.

Not long after, the public gardens at Dumbarton Oaks in Washington's Georgetown provided for me the same kind of private estate. I walked every inch of those magnificent terraces in every season. I drank in sunshine and the beauty of both the formal gardens and the acres of country meadows. I have never forgotten those days and was delighted these many years later to learn through an article for *Victoria* of the landscaping of Dumbarton Oaks by Beatrix Farrand. Knowing the garden's origins and discovering that it was a woman designer who produced such a masterpiece have made my recollections even more meaningful.

I am especially proud that this collection of "moments in the garden" includes Cranbrook House in Bloomfield Hills, Michigan. These beautifully groomed grounds, the work of dedicated volunteers, were precious to me when my son attended nearby Cranbrook School during his high school years. We would walk over the gardens on each visit; most often our talk was of happy times and typical school-

boy matters. But on occasion we talked through a problem of growing-up years, the dense greenery muffling the pain a young boy was feeling. Now we return with a mature young man treading beside us and the grounds of Cranbrook House give us all a quiet peace and understanding.

And so, as Colette suggests, many a garden has left its memory on me—even if I have only viewed them on our pages through the incomparable photography of Toshi Otsuki. Toshi is not only a photographer with the infinite patience to understand a garden before he records it, he is always a gentleman visitor. With the finest manners he enters and moves about, and I always think that because of this impeccable behavior, flowers, birds, and all inhabitants appear to stand still and also behave with corresponding dignity for his camera. Here, his visual eloquence is married to a fine text by Tovah Martin, whose words guide us to poignant recollections and whose careful observations will please garden enthusiasts. Tovah's sensibilities, like those of Toshi's, remind us of a heritage we at *Victoria* strive to preserve—a heritage of beauty and of honoring caring people.

Nancy Lindemeyer
New York City
Spring, 1991

Breathtaking views await at the Gardens of Cranbrook House.

A Quiet Moment at the Huntington

An early spring sunset is framed against the arboretum's graceful branches, above. On the pedestal of a gurgling fountain, a whimsical angel contemplates the scene, opposite.

And in the thickest covert of that shade
There was a pleasant arbor, not by art,
But of the trees owne inclination made . . .

Edmund Spenser

FOUR SEASONS OF SPLENDOR
BLITHEWOLD GARDENS AND ARBORETUM

*I*n an early spring afternoon, the sun slips gently through the branches to illuminate an ocean of daffodils at Blithewold, an arboretum in Bristol, Rhode Island. For a moment, Blithewold's bosquet is ablaze with color. Thousands of daffodils flock between the trees, roaming the woods in brilliant battalions.

Meanwhile, up above, the trees are donning their summer plumage. By mid-May, the daffodils will disappear and the bosquet will be dominated by trees. Overhead, lindens, Norway maples, and European ash become lush and leafy. Gradually, almost unnoticed, the bosquet is transformed from a sun-washed, flower-filled place into a shadowy, half-hidden glade. In the heat of the summer, curly creeping ivy, aegopodium, and vinca carpet the ground where daffodils once waltzed, and a cool canopy of deep green branches casts dappled shade over the entire scene.

After the first flush of spring, Blithewold settles into sylvan pursuits. Although flower beds stretch here and there on the estate, they play counterpoint

At Blithewold, April belongs to the daffodils. Nearly thirty thousand bulbs run nimbly amongst lindens, Norway maples, and European ash.

Lover's Lane cuts a path among the trees straight down to the water.

While spring is still shivering in sea breezes, the daffodils glisten golden in the sun.

to the arboretum. Some truly rare sylvan specimens interlace leaves at Blithewold, bending lithely in the sea breezes, rustling to the music of the ocean.

Originally Blithewold was the summer home of the Van Wickle family, purchased in 1894 merely as a mooring for their newly purchased steam yacht. But after devoting a few summers solely to nautical pleasures, the family turned its attention toward improving the sprawling acreage surrounding their forty-five room "cottage" close to the bay in Bristol. Even then the most visible element of the estate was its majestic trees. A landscape designer was engaged to enhance the resident saplings, and so the arboretum began.

With passing years, the sylvan passion grew stronger. When house guests arrived at the summer cottage, they often came bearing arboreal hospitality gifts, and the family returned from abroad laden with botanical souvenirs. As a result, rare arboreal aristocrats such as Sargent's weeping hemlock (*Tsuga canadensis* 'Pendula'), the Franklin tree (*Franklinia alatamaha*), the maidenhair tree (*Ginkgo biloba*), and the Japanese stewartia (*Stewartia pseudocamellia*) are silhouetted by Bristol Harbor.

Towering head and shoulders above them all, presiding pompously over the grounds with a kingly presence, stretches an immense, eighty-five-foot sequoia (*Sequoiadendrom giganteum*), the tallest on the East Coast. Ever since that grand sequoia came to Blithewold as a twelve-foot fledgling in 1911, it has been pampered and protected by lightning rods as the brittle branches reach skyward. Hurricanes have wreaked havoc with neighboring trees, but the giant sequoia stands firm. Now Blithewold boasts a nursery of twelve younger sequoias, all contemplatively overlooking Narragansett Bay.

Texture and form provide the resounding themes at Blithewold, explored again and again in all their many arboreal nuances. Trees clad in vastly different plumage parade down the entry drive leading to the mansion, and they also link branches in a square surrounding a large side lawn. With space aplenty for expanding girth and stretching limbs, the Japanese cedar (*Cryptomeria japonica*) rubs shoulders beside a Carolina allspice (*Calycanthus floridus*), while the lacy foliage of the umbrella pine (*Sciadopitys verticillata*) complements the giant sequoia's sharp profile.

The arboretum is not entirely a symphony in green. Here and there amongst a smattering of

Punctuating the procession of trees on the front lawn, a Colonial Revival well house sits surrounded by benches. Later in the season, climbing pink roses will entwine its columns.

seasonal sylvan blooms, flower beds also bask by the water. As spring slips into summer, the intense rays reflected from the ocean nurture spectacular cutting and vegetable gardens cultivated to provide the mansion with armloads of bouquets and a cornucopia of succulent fruit for hearty feasts. A continuous border of impeccably clipped lavender cotton (*Santolina chamaecyparissus*) appears to rein in the vivid blossoms, preventing them from rushing pell-mell into the nearby glasshouse. Undulating in waves around the rectangular lily pond, riotous zinnias, drumstick onions (*Allium giganteum*), and glowing yarrow look all the more sensational within their prim silver-clipped corral.

The path from the sun-kissed cutting garden proceeds into the shadow-filled bosquet with its somber hues and contemplative benches. Compared to the surrounding yawning lawns, the bosquet is a secret place where birds might alight on a statue and confidences can be shared in solitude. And the digression is all the more delicious because it is

A serious-faced statue, perhaps of Socrates, proudly surveys the daffodil-studded scene while an early-season robin ruffles his feathers against the chill morning air.

merely a momentary diversion. When the path emerges again, it revels in the bedazzling bright tones of blue and yellow flower beds tucked beside the mansion's stone wall. *Hydrangea anomala petiolaris* drapes the masonry with the opulence of lush verdure and ivory lace-cap blossoms. Just in front of the wall, with feathery spires that lightly brush the hydrangea in a breeze, delphiniums are protected from the whipping winds rushing off the water to stand straight and tall. At their feet, yellow and blue perennials and annuals form neat clumps of color carefully combined to reflect the hues of the sparkling sea. Purple mounds of *Nepeta* × *faassenii* and spikes of aromatic lavender impart their perfume to the air. Saucy, sun-ray yellow dahlias shimmer like luminaries amongst a bed of green foliage. And all the many blues of the ocean are echoed in the campanula, lobelia, and Siberian iris. Later, lemon daylilies dance on tall stems in the background.

The garden rounds a bend to look outward toward ten acres of neatly mown greensward overlooking Bristol Harbor. At the farther end of the great lawn, almost on the edge of the sea, a turf bridge crosses a pond amidst an Oriental garden. In understated majesty, a petite Japanese maple spreads its dainty boughs beside a pagoda and a meditative boulder. Nearby, on the other side of the bridge, a rock garden cradles alpines nestled in their stone crevices only feet from the water's edge.

Blithewold has a rustic demeanor. From the nimble daffodils of spring through the rambling roses of summer, the gardens skip lightly across the seasons. Comfortable garden benches are composed simply of piled stones cushioned in a soft bed of ivy. Bridges are sheathed in turf, and fences are fashioned of local stone. Blithewold is the sort of place that invites a barefoot dash down the lawn.

A Garden in Crystal

Clustered under a cloche, the resident freesia has a perfume that can be discovered only by lifting the lid.

$\mathcal{A}$ glass case often stood solemnly amidst the deep mahogany furniture in the Victorian front parlor. Through its misty panes, the silhouette of a salubrious fern was vaguely discernible groping its fronds against the leaded seams. A gesneriad, an orchid, and perhaps a begonia or two opened gay blossoms inside, but their brilliant buds were transformed into opaque splashes seen from the far side of the foggy panes. The true contents of the case could be identified only by raising the hinged glass lid and peering inside.

When the lid was opened, a rush of moist, warm air escaped, laden with its wonderful medley of mingled scents both earthy and floral. But the elixir was rarely allowed to escape. The lid of a Wardian Case was raised only for a moment and scarcely more. Then the brass hinges were snapped shut, sealing the delicate tropicals once again in the rarified atmosphere of a crystal world, protected from the capricious climate in the parlor.

Born of a love of botany, glass cases were the brainchild of Nathaniel Ward, a prosperous London physician and an ardent naturalist. When weather permitted, he took to the country, collecting ferns and netting insects for closer scrutiny in his spare time. Alas, upon his return, the collected plants invariably perished in the polluted city air. Unable to maintain live plants in London, Dr. Ward confined his interaction with nature solely to occasional country outings until, on one such excursion in 1830, he happened upon a hawkmoth chrysalis and sealed it in a glass jar to await metamorphosis. Six months later, the doctor was contemplating his sleeping cocoon when he discovered a male fern sporeling *(Dryopteris filix-mas)* thriving in the sealed-glass environment. At last, he had unearthed a means of cultivating ferns—and anything else he might collect—in his city home. Being a humanitarian at heart, the physician shared his discovery with other city-bound nature lovers. Before

Through the misty glass, the bright pink shades of the diminutive elfin herb Cuphea hyssopifolia *interlace with the buds of* Streptocarpus *'Little Gem'.*

From a distance, the world inside a Wardian case is a blur of intermingling colors.

long, Wardian cases (as they were called) found their way into nearly every British parlor, and from there the fashion floated over to the United States.

Glass gardens were crafted in all shapes and forms. Most often, a simple glass dome was fitted tightly over a clay pot. Modest cases had four straight sides and a hinged top which could be swung open to admire the miniature landscape captive in those misty walls. But, inevitably, whimsy took flight. Before long, the parlor began sprouting small-scale renditions of Kew Gardens, the Crystal Palace, Japanese pagodas, and all sorts of other architectural wonders crafted

deftly of glass.

British Wardian cases generally held native ferns captive in their moisture-frosted walls, but American gardeners preferred to harbor tiny tropical rarities in their glass enclosures. Captive in the contained case, an incumbent's thirst was quenched by the droplets of water on the glass. A world in miniature could survive in a Wardian case for months with very little care. And to keep insects at bay, a salamander or toad was often invited to become lord of his own crystal kingdom. Like a globe on its pedestal, a miniature world lay locked in the Wardian case, waiting for someone to take a closer look.

Two by two, American hornbeam hedges part only for a moment to allow a glimpse, above, at the Provencal fountain in the center of the Ellipse. Dumbarton's Rose Garden is a rhapsody in muted colors. 'Peace' is a popular hybrid tea, opposite, with its creamy white color with frosted pink edging.

In my garden I spend my days;
In my library I spend my nights.

Alexander Smith

BEATRIX FARRAND, "THIS GRAND ART OF MINE"
DUMBARTON OAKS

There is a place in Georgetown, not far from the nation's Capitol, where the bustle of the city is muffled in a flush of greenery. Hidden behind a high brick wall, it is a place where a long afternoon can be spent wandering spellbound through garden after garden and still many secret venues will remain unexplored. Lying just beyond an imposing wrought iron gate, this is a kingdom where gracefully curved drives open into secluded courtyards, verdant paths beckon from every side, and walkways lead to enchanted cata-combs embraced by blossoms.

Dumbarton Oaks waits to be discovered. Carved from a perilous hill rolling down to a trickling arm of the Potomac River, the estate portrays many themes and many moods, all interwoven harmoniously on sixteen blissful acres. Enclosed in its solid brick wall, a series of secret gardens resides.

At first glance pomp and ceremony seem to reign, but formality dissolves into warm familiarity as the garden gleefully disperses into many formal "rooms." Each annex carries its own theme: one

Framed in the branches of the estate's oldest tree, a black oak (Quercus velutina), *the Green Garden Terrace surveys Dumbarton Heights.* I'd LOVE to visit Dumbarton Oaks

in PERSON. What a glorious trip it would be.

nook holds chrysanthemums, a shady alcove protects impatiens, and still another chamber is redolent of roses. And yet, despite different personalities, all are connected by a common charm and a series of nearly identical Portuguese garden sheds.

Dumbarton Oaks invites wandering, but it never reveals all its varied facets; a mystery lies beyond every bend. This perfect garden was just a glimmer when Robert and Mildred Bliss purchased Dumbarton Oaks in 1920. Weary of the nomadic life of diplomats, the ambassador and his wife needed a pied-à-terre near downtown Washington. Discriminating collectors of art, patrons of music, and ardent lovers of nature, the couple wanted to create an oasis of culture. Realizing no ordinary landscape architect could fulfill their dream of mingling of nature and art, they invited Beatrix Jones Farrand to design the estate.

As a child, young Beatrix was called "the Earthshaker" by Henry James, who often visited her family. The novelist's light-hearted jibe was, in fact, an accurate prediction. The precocious Beatrix Jones designed a garden for her family at age eleven. Talented in music, adept at art, and endowed with a brilliant intellect, she chose to pursue the field of horticulture from the very start, and her strong will paved the way. Somehow, she managed to become an apprentice to the famous professor Charles Sargent at Harvard University's Arnold Arboretum, treading a path which few women had previously explored. Before her twenty-fifth birthday, Beatrix had become one of the first female landscape gardeners in this country, and perhaps the greatest. For those aghast at her chosen vocation, she answered, "With this grand art of mine, I do not envy the greatest painter or sculptor or poet that lived. It seems to me that all arts are combined in this."

As a sole spark of color amidst greenery, a climbing rose is trained to caress an urn.

So Beatrix Farrand was already well-established in 1922, when, at the age of fifty, she forged her friendship with Mildred Bliss and came to Dumbarton Oaks to survey the grounds. Together, they saw a mutual vision for the garden. The "noble elements" steering the design were the magnificent trees stretching their limbs all around the estate. The stately katsura *(Cercidiphyllum japonicum)*, Japanese maple *(Acer palmatum)*, American beech *(Fagus grandifolia)*, and black oak *(Quercus velutina)* lent character to the land—and that personality was to be preserved. Flowers were to be added only to enhance and accentuate the grandeur of the trees. And, of course, the steep lay of the land also ruled the garden's architecture. From the woods and slopes, the gardens of Dumbarton Oaks slowly emerged and flourished.

The grand trees were incorporated as "markers" to frame a view or blend into the chorus of colors. Terraces would scale the steep slope of the land—the lowest garden lying a full fifty-five feet below the uppermost balcony. But before a single sapling was felled or a meager mound was leveled, Beatrix Farrand took time to develop an intimacy with the land that she would mold. Season after season she "listened to the light and wind and grade of each area." All the while, her friendship with the Blisses grew until she knew their tastes and pleasures as well as she knew the feel of the land.

Finally, the moment was ripe to begin the transformation of naked woods and rolling hills into a deftly conceived design. And, mercifully, the Blisses were assigned to diplomatic service in Sweden while Dumbarton Oaks was in upheaval. During their absence, earth was moved cartload by cartload to form the cluster of terraces. Pipes were laid and drainage ditches were installed. The Blisses returned periodically to witness the progress. Even while they were overseas, mockups of every pavilion, urn, and fountain were photographed and sent for the Blisses' approval.

Throughout the metamorphosis, Beatrix Farrand was always present—revising, measuring, and listening—as the land was molded into shape. At last, the terraces were laid, leveled, and prepared for planting. Everyone awaited further orders. But when the time came, no plans were unfurled and handed to the head gardener. Instead, Mrs. Farrand met each caretaker personally with a stack of wooden plant labels in her hands. Together, they positioned the labels in the soil to plot where each perennial, shrub, and tree would settle in.

What emerged was the persona of Dumbarton Oaks, a place where wisteria and clematis festoon loggias surrounding glistening terraces, while flowering fruit trees sweep their branches just inches from sparkling pools. Long, sweeping herbaceous borders lead the visitor from one verdant room to another. And everywhere are tucked benches and garden seats so that guests may enjoy a few minutes immersed in contemplation. It is a garden to share, but also a very personal place. Beside Mildred Bliss's favorite bench, Mrs. Farrand thoughtfully fitted a book box to be filled with oft-read volumes ready for a quiet moment.

The gardens surrounding the house are strictly structured. Hedges are clipped, lines are sharply geometric, and formality rules the realm. Farther out, perennials sprawl easily in beds, and roving yellow blooming jasmine *(Jasminum nudiflorum)* and wisteria interlace fingers. Finally, on the edge of the estate, the gardens disperse into wandering paths flanking sun-drenched, glistening forsythia dells or skirting the confetti texture of a pink dappled cherry orchard. Farther afield, where design plays softly with nature's own wild and rampant ways, the plantings appear informal but are always carefully premeditated. The artwork is all precisely balanced. The geometry of the paths offsetting plants, the balance of trees counterpoised with sky is all carefully weighed to impart a delicious, restful equilibrium. And yet, just as a ballet's choreography is soon overshadowed by the ballerina's grace, so the wild areas Forsythia Hill, Cherry Hill, and Melisande's Allée all impart the impression that

The Urn Garden captivates with its modest monochromatic design, yet it was designed primarily as a fanfare announcing and overlooking the Rose Garden below.

nature is performing entirely unfettered. Although deftly planned and painstakingly executed, a wonderful flush-faced spontaneity prevails throughout the gardens at Dumbarton Oaks.

Two decades passed before Dumbarton Oaks was finished. It was, in Mildred Bliss's words, "the sort of place in which thrushes sing and dreams are dreamt." In 1940, the Blisses decided to preserve their personal paradise for posterity and gave Dumbarton Oaks to Harvard University. They *what WONDERFUL people!* moved to a home not far away, so that they could return to visit their garden and watch as it continued to flourish. Half a century later, the garden still looks as if Beatrix Farrand just finished carefully tying a wisp of wisteria firmly onto its arbor.

Dumbarton Oaks remains perfectly locked in time. To one treading up the circular gravel drive, the stately Georgian home, standing prominently on

The Fountain Terrace is surrounded with snapdragons, dahlias, foxglove and lively annuals.

An eighteenth-century lead fountain cavorts in the center of its terrace.

Potted plants from the orangery bask in the sun of the Arbor Terrace.

its perch at the crest of Dumbarton Heights, presents a serious and formal facade. Snuggled under its east wing stretches an ornate orangery built in 1810, veiled in springtime by a confetti of pristine silver blossoms showering from *Magnolia heptapeta*. Each arched window is framed by the feathery foliage and opulent, grapelike floral clusters of wisteria filtering the sun's stronger rays in midsummer but permitting the light to spill through the panes unobstructed during the darker, colder months. Throughout the winter, oleander, tibouchina, gardenia, citrus, and brunfelsia perform in their warm, cozy, light-splashed home. In summer, the potted tropicals move onto the porch, leaving the century-old creeping fig *(Ficus pumila)* alone in the orangery to wander around the walls, sending forth gnarled branches to form a delightful soft sculpture

Flanked with snapdragons, the gate to the Arbor Terrace stands invitingly ajar.

A series of Portuguese-style garden sheds adds continuity to this garden of many "rooms."

in front of the sparkling windows.

The tropicals spend their summer sojourn enjoying the view from the uppermost terrace, a garden composed solely in varying shades of green. Small-leaved ivy roams on the north walls, where wisteria would never form buds, and *Jasminum nudiflorum*, the winter-blooming jasmine, climbs amongst scalloped ferns on the fence. Standing supreme above all, a venerable black oak, *Quercus velutina*—the oldest tree on the estate—still spreads its limbs not far from the window where Mildred Bliss once sat at her writing desk.

The terrace was composed to frame vivacious, bubbling evening parties. But not far away, a more intimate "room" awaits those who prefer a quiet tête-à-tête. This is the Zodiac Garden, where a star is set in the stone floor. Encased in a white aromatic cloud of *Rhododendron mucronatum* in spring and in the

spice-scented, snowy blossoms of *Clematis paniculata* in autumn, a cozy bench waits for two to exchange confidences. Below, the Aquarius fountain empties a water jug one drip at a time into a basin.

At Dumbarton Oaks, surprises lurk at the foot of every stairway and sprawl at the turn of every bend. The Zodiac Garden opens unexpectedly into a grand promenade stretching like a lengthy shadow from the house. The North Vista is a symphony in green. A velvety expanse of immaculately clipped greensward framed in twin deodar cedars *(Cedrus deodara)* slopes gently downward in what appears to be a seamless lawn sweeping into oblivion. In fact, it is an ingenious architectural illusion: grassy steps, hidden by their slope, scale the hill; their tapered edging cleverly lengthens the view.

Many paths lead from the North Vista. On one hand, walkways wander into the contemplative ave-

Reminiscent of an English cottage garden, a long, colorful herbaceous border runs down the slope toward Melisande's Allée.

nues of Crabapple Hill, where an orchard of sculpted trees blushes with a profusion of pink blossoms every spring. Further along, Mildred Bliss's favorite "celestial meadows" await when the glistening, golden Forsythia Dell bursts into blossom. Everywhere benches sit ready to revive weary wanderers as they travel amidst the flora.

Take another route from the North Vista, and the walkway leads through a maze of formal rooms that lure and tease coquettishly at every corner. An overlook reveals a refreshing swimming pool skirted by a wisteria-embowered loggia. A few steps below, the famous Pebble Garden displays its shimmering mosaic. Originally a tennis court, the Pebble Garden now depicts the wheat sheath and cornucopia pattern symbolizing the Bliss motto, "As you sow, so shall you reap." Composed in the subtle shades of Mexican stone moistened to a glistening shimmer by

This herbaceous border displays a rare burst of color—pink, red, and sky blue—by combining snapdragons and flax.

In summer, the orangery is emptied of potted plants.

a shallow film of water, the mosaic is enhanced and defined by raised beds of sedum, thyme, and portulaca highlighting the scrollwork.

Around a corner waits a deep green avenue of clipped boxwood leading down, and then down again, while a fountain beckons somewhere in the distance. Then, suddenly, the path opens into a sun-drenched courtyard revealing the illusive, illuminated central fountain, which stands just ahead washed in a field of light, surrounded by a double circle of clipped American hornbeams *(Carpinus caroliniana)*. Marching two by two, the naked trunks of the hornbeam permit sun to penetrate while their aerial hedge encircles the space in formal pageantry.

More paths lead to more gardens. Gates stand invitingly ajar and then brandish breathtaking plantings where colors, textures, and forms are all ingeniously selected, all in rich accord. Terraces seem to overhang precipices until another terrace suddenly appears—as if by magic—a few steps below.

A series of Portuguese-style garden sheds descends the hill to the east of the house. They house the tools of the trade and maintain fluidity in the scene. They also add an ounce of whimsy to the "working" gardens where chrysanthemums wait in their nursery until blooming time is nigh. Each shed raises its head from a lower level, so the visitor might catch a quick whiff of the tuberoses or nicotiana that dwell in the beds below.

The gardens alternate ravishing color with subdued shades. The Urn Terrace is a tapestry of counterpoised monochromatics: the lush lawn is accented by spiraling paisley beds of darkest ivy all glorifying a single pedestal. But this somber scene is orchestrated merely to set the stage for the Rose Garden below. As one looks down, a spread of sumptuous pastel shades intermingles and blends

The formal gardens near the Dumbarton Oaks mansion boast brick paths. But as the gardens wander further from the house and escape into informality, the walkways change character; they are paved with stone.

In the Forsythia Dell, nature encroaches on the workings of man as vines battle to win territory. Everywhere, seats stand ready for a contemplative moment.

beautifully. All the while, perfume rises from a thousand intensely aromatic blossoms.

From the Rose Garden, the Fountain Terrace opens forth with its cavorting cherubs splashing mischievously in shallow pools. Originally, Dumbarton Oaks was designed as a garden for only three seasons—the Blisses were not in residence in midsummer. In the Fountain Terrace, tulips were planted for spring entertainment, and chrysanthemums put on an autumn extravaganza. In winter, the stately trees outlined a garden of silhouettes. Now, the grounds have been choreographed to continue throughout the year. Bulbs are followed by bright annuals and perennials in cheerful primary colors until the muted shades of maroon, copper, and golden chrysanthemums are ready to take the stage.

From those cultivated pleasures, the gardens

Overlooking the Lover's Lane Pool, an arbor holds honeysuckle and provides a backdrop for a series of grassy seats.

Professor Sargent grew impatient with Beatrix, ranting, "Don't waste time on what you call design . . . there is no time to sit on benches; a tree stump will do as well."

again slip into wildness as Melisande's Allée departs into the woods. The roving path meanders seemingly aimlessly, lined by a tunnel of silver maples *(Acer saccharinum)* shading the way. But, of course, a surprise awaits. The walkway suddenly swells into a clearing accented by an oval reflecting pool encased in the ferny foliage of lacy bamboo. Originally designed as an outdoor theater, the area has a series of cushiony, grassy seats overlooking the still water in contemplative serenity. In a labyrinth of many secret places, this is the most intimate. From the still water of the pond, the front gate and the busy street beyond seem very far away.

Dumbarton Oaks has a complexity that unravels only with familiarity. This is a place of promises proffered and finally fulfilled. It is a garden that shares secrets and offers insights. Like a close friendship, it grows more beautiful with time.

A Thousand Roses in Residence

*I*f the air is still and the sun is shining, a delightful perfume floats enticingly through the orangery windows at Dumbarton Oaks. The scent lures the visitor closer and still closer, down the steps into the Urn Terrace, searching for its origin. Finally, standing on an overlook, the visitor discovers the source of the aroma. There, spread in a delicious tapestry of carefully combined colors, lies the Rose Garden, clad in a thousand vibrant blossoms sending a mingled scent upward.

There are many sights to be seen at Dumbarton Oaks; innumerable vistas wait to captivate a visitor's eye. But in a place overflowing with surprises, the Rose Garden dazzles above all. Suddenly, terraces above and below are merely a prelude to the Rose Garden's grand crescendo. Throughout the season, the beds are carpeted in a plush brocade of color. Square beds, triangular beds, horseshoe-shaped beds—each bed holds its own special rose. In one bed, 'Mrs. Pierre S. du Pont' opens her golden buds to reveal a fluffy nest of stamens. Not far away, 'Tiffany' sends forth a rich fragrance from her peach-tinged lips. Each hue is segregated. A rainbow rules this garden, and yet, a restful atmosphere prevails. Color is everywhere, but the muted shades are never overpowering. Outlined by grassy avenues, the colors are clarified. Silhouetted against carefully pruned boxwood topiary, they gain vibrancy.

Of all the gardens at Dumbarton Oaks, the Rose Garden boasts the broadest spectrum of color. Mildred Bliss disapproved of the racier shades of mauve and magenta, banishing them from Dumbarton's grounds. But, in the Rose Garden, she permitted Beatrix Farrand to play with a full palette of shades. Although given liberty to combine colors as she so desired, the landscape gardener cautiously brought in the brighter hues only to accent and add depth to her design.

At the entrance to the Rose Garden are subtle pink and salmon shades deepened by magentas thrown in for spice. Then, near the center, the spectrum moves toward salmon and yellow before simmering into gold and pale orange in the farthest reaches of the enclosure. Surrounding the beds of neatly pruned bush roses, energetic ramblers with legendary names such as 'American Pillar' and 'Frau Karl Druschki' climb the stone walls, leaning their flower-laden branches informally wherever they can find elbow room.

Originally, Beatrix Farrand planted a combination of tea and hybrid tea roses in her geometric beds. 'Mme. Butterfly', 'Golden Dawn', 'Red Radiance', and all the latest novelties of the 1920s could be found basking, each in its own bed. The modern tea roses were favored over heirloom varieties because they would provide the long-lasting impact that Dumbarton Oaks—the diplomatic garden—demanded. Carefully selected modern roses have all the subtlety of antique hybrids, but they unfurl their

In muted glory, the Rose Garden now blossoms throughout the season with its aromatic hybrid tea roses budding amongst boxwood.

bounty of buds on and on for months at a time. Then, there was the serious matter of the flowers' health to consider. When a thousand roses are in residence, their upkeep becomes an important factor. Modern roses display resistance to mildew as well as other rose-related ills. They have all the poetry of heirloom varieties, but none of the peevishness. So antique roses roamed the walls, but the beds were planted with hybrid teas and edged with sternly clipped boxwood (*Buxus sempervirens* 'Suffruticosa'), modestly hiding the rose's thorny ankles. To enhance the green foil, mounds of boxwood waded in among the roses here and there, while a giant spiral boxwood was proudly positioned to reign in the center.

The design was heavenly; it was a brilliant combination of color and foliar texture. But, alas, the boxwood and roses proved to be poor bedfellows. The evergreens fared badly during the damp Washington winters, and the hedges formed a barricade halting the flow of air to the roses. Moving air is a rose's life blood; it prevents mildew and blights from settling on those most finicky of flowers. Although perched on a steep slope with

well-drained soil underfoot, both roses and boxwoods pouted pitifully. The garden was redesigned in 1970 with bluestone paving rather than boxwood for edging. Some of the lushness was lost, but the loss was more than repaid in the brilliance of the rose blossoms. Finally, the flowers smiled unhampered. Improved hybrid teas—chosen to remain faithful to the original aura of colors—now bloom abundantly throughout the entire season, sending their intoxicating combined perfume wandering throughout the adjacent terraces. The last rose

of summer does not spill its petals until December.

Against the east wall sprawls a very comfortable, radiantly white stone bench, offering respite for those who come to partake of the perfume. This was Mildred Bliss's favorite perch, amidst a sea of delicate color. She loved the Rose Garden above every other room in her enchanted kingdom. Choreographed to capture a moment of lush color, the Rose Garden spends the entire summer blushed in shades of sunrise.

'Jubilant' features lush salmon buds.

Pink edges make 'Peace' distinctive.

'Peace' is glorious from any angle.

The all-pink blossom of 'Tiffany' makes it a favorite.

Emily Dickinson, with her dog at her side, would walk the straight path past the orchard to worship nature in her perennial garden.

Some keep the Sabbath going to Church—
I keep it, staying at Home—
With a Bobolink for a Chorister—
And an Orchard for a Dome—

Emily Dickinson

A POET'S PRIVATE PLACE
THE EMILY DICKINSON HOMESTEAD

A flagstone walkway leads to the garden of one of the greatest poets in American literature, the Belle of Amherst, Emily Dickinson.

Beckoning from the east porch of the old Federal style home, the flagstones march straight and single file past the lonesome oak, down the hill. The path proceeds unbroken, unwavering, never pausing until the stones touch the garden's edge.

Then, when the garden is nearly within reach, when vintage roses tease your senses with perfume and aromatic artemisias beg to be fondled, the walk suddenly takes a turn and dissolves into stepping stones. It skips down the bank in hops and jumps.

At the garden's edge, the path disappears down a set of stone steps and expands into a grassy square surrounded on every side by billowing, blossom-filled beds. A retrospective garden is shaded by the same oak that spread its limbs protectively over Emily Dickinson's flowery domain. Restored by Amherst College in 1972, the Dickinson garden is planted with flowers similar to those that inspired the poet in the 1850s.

A subdued garden surrounds the grassy square. A medley of moody indigos, quiet pinks, and soft silvers entwines the immaculately edged, rectangular beds. The design might be simple, but the plantings are not. Each bed holds an eclectic combination of different perennials, each closely shouldering its neighbors in the voluptuous, overbrimming, jigsaw style that was very much in vogue. Emily may have rebelled against fashion in many ways—she refused to wear the bright colors popular in the nineteenth century and, as the years passed, dressed only in pure white—but her garden was delightfully conventional. The abundant beds that hem the neatly clipped meridian could be comfortable beside any home in Amherst.

But this is no ordinary garden. It is a poet's retreat, thoughtfully planted as an artist carefully fills a canvas. The garden is a place of inspiration, meant to be admired from all angles. Its perennials interlace so seamlessly that one color spills into the next while shapes entwine. Foxgloves stand in stately spires nestled closely beside stout purple eupatorium. Here and there white phlox and silver artemisia shine so luminously that Emily might have seen them glistening in the moonlight long after dark as she sat on the large east porch. Textures interplay. The lacy leaves of daisies are accented by the sharp, swordlike blades of irises.

A tall, plump hemlock, skirted on both sides by blue-green junipers, stands in one corner of the beds, providing a hefty anchor for the design. The stately hemlock gives the scene height while the junipers pick up the blues in the garden and tie them restfully together. There are no arresting elements here. The garden is a fluid, quietly serene place. No single flower steals the show. Instead, the

Proud delphiniums stand head and shoulders above the other blooms in the perennial garden.

Sidalcea 'Jimmy Whitelet' stands three to four feet tall with a crown of pink-etched flowers throughout the summer.

Pristine white lilies sparkle in the daylight and glow after dark in the moonlight .

blooms form a chorus to proclaim in unison, "Nature is Harmony— / Nature is what we know—."

The Belle of Amherst knew nature intimately. The garden sits on the outer boundary of Emily Dickinson's world. In her mid-thirties, the poet decided, "I do not cross my Father's ground to any House or town." Following that self-induced seclusion, she left home only twice. She lived for two decades content to travel no further than the meadow beyond her garden.

Only a few very dear friends shared Emily's life. Instead, she socialized with the daisies and the foxglove. In the poet's own words, "The Soul selects her own Society— / Then—shuts the Door—." The garden, the meadow, the birds, and the insects were Emily Dickinson's most intimate companions.

Thus, the reclusive poet planted her small gar-den as a reposeful haven and a place of solitude. The square of blossoms is buffered on one side by a screen of bush honeysuckles and venerable rhodo-dendrons, while a massive thicket of hemlock shelters it from the street. Not far away, on a breezy knoll beside the barnyard, a barricade of lilacs "sway with purple load." Above, the oak tree and a giant *Magnolia tripetala* spread their umbrellalike fo-liage, giving the garden a ceiling.

Immersed in her sunken garden, safely hidden on all sides by blossoms, Emily spent many blissful hours. In moments when she was not baking gin-gerbread or attending to the dozens of domestic duties that undoubtedly preoccupied her time, Emily could be found bending her knees on a care-fully folded woolen blanket, pulling weeds or pluck-ing spent blossoms.

Emily Dickinson's Natural Paradise

The tree-studded meadow between the old brick home and her garden enthralled Emily just as much as her flower garden did.

A white geranium flourishes in the south window of Emily's room.

Emily's garden is still faithfully orchestrated to feature unceasing entertainment. In spring, the garden bursts with an enthusiasm of bulbs. The hyacinth "puts out a Ruffled Head," and *Narcissus* 'Thalia' and 'Ice Follies' blare their cheerful white trumpets, while gay tulips dance nearby. In April, a cacophony of colors dances rakishly in the beds.

By June, the garden has mellowed into coral epimediums and fluffy early peonies bedded in a sea of shy violets. Then come summer's lilies, spires of blue delphinium interspersed with the cool pinks of sidalcea, physostegia (the false dragonhead), and foxglove with pastel daylilies scattered about. And, of course, roses unfold their porcelain blossoms close to the garden's border. They reside purposely within easy reach to facilitate the primping and care

that roses demand. A jar of kerosene still sits partially hidden by the rose foliage, filled with beetles plucked by a gardener early in the morning.

As the season wears on, the garden gains height as well as girth until the foxglove nearly touches the leafy branches of the old oak tree that sends dappled shade throughout. When summer begins to slip into autumn, when "The berry's cheek is plumper— / The Rose is out of town," the Dickinson garden is still lusty. Phlox opens its perfumed umbels amidst the purple plumes of *Salvia farinacea* and the airy blooms of frilly asters. All the while, golden black-eyed Susans and yellow *Coreopsis verticillata* 'Moonbeam' echo the hues of the maple tree not far away, while the blue cups of *Campanula carpatica* pick up the shades of the crisp sky. Emily's autumnal garden holds "the nosegays of twilight" late in the year.

When the snows fall in Amherst, the square garden disappears underneath its blanket, leaving only the hemlock and juniper cradling a contemplative low stone bench. From the house, the garden's sunken outline is just visible and the evergreens stand as a promise of more colorful seasons to come.

The square of blossoms was not Emily's only garden. She spent long hours in the meadow leading up to the old brick house. At a time before machinery mowed meadows clean, the large field skirting the Dickinson homestead was filled with the "Dandelion's pallid tube" as well as quantities of sweet-bloomed clover to entertain the appetites of humming bees. Nature was a stage filled with an ever-changing drama. Even the dancing blades of grass kindled the poet's ecstasy. All was observed, all was held in her mind's eye. And, after dark, the Belle of Amherst slipped quietly up to her room to faithfully record—in perfect meter—the theatrics of the day.

Tucked in a shady spot, the double rue anemone (Anemonella thalictroides 'Schoaf's Double') opens its magenta blossoms amidst a lacework of greenery.

. . . the bounty of earth itself, assumes a calculus of art above the mathematics and genius of man.

David McCord
from the plaque at the Garden in the Woods entry

A PRESERVING NATURE
THE WILL C. CURTIS GARDEN IN THE WOODS

A path meanders through the woods. It plunges into sudden valleys and climbs to mount steep hillocks; it encircles still ponds and crosses rushing creeks. No brick walks or straight lines traverse the Garden in the Woods. No travertine statues or gurgling fountains are to be found within its boundaries. In this garden, rambling gravel paths weave leisurely through wooded bogs and descend into steep kettles studded with blossoming wildflowers. Man's hand is hardly felt.

The Garden in the Woods was born in 1931 when Will Curtis, who preferred to call himself a naturalistic landscaper rather than a designer, happened to be bouncing along the back roads of Sudbury and Framingham, Massachusetts, on a Sunday drive. He spotted hints of an intriguing forest and set out to explore it on foot. It was a landscaper's dream. Here was the perfect place to integrate wildlings and exotic species in a natural setting. He purchased the thirty-acre plot from a railroad company; working softly with nature, he built a garden from the woods.

Using the forest as a theme, Curtis and his assistant, Howard "Dick" Stiles, added flowering shrubs to give the landscape color, and underplanted with

Catching the sun rays scattered between the trees, ivory lily-of-the-field (Anemone canadensis) *turns its cups toward the light.*

*As the sun filters through the trees, it caresses the filigree of
a bracken fern* (Pteridium aquilinum).

*Breaking through the soil in springtime, the young
fiddleheads of the cinnamon fern are delicious to nibble.*

roving wildlings to carpet the ground. They portrayed the forest in its most complimentary light. Species and hybrids were carefully interplanted, and native shrubs and hardy foreign species were placed side by side, forming a fantastic liaison. They created the gentlest possible form of chaos. Often, Stiles labored by lantern light until midnight to finish planting shrubs before inclement weather broke. Through foul winters and a ravaging tornado, through brilliant springs and dramatic autumns, the two maintained the gardens until old age put an end to Curtis's landscaping income. When the partners could no longer afford to maintain their Garden in the Woods, they gave the land to the New England Wild Flower Society to establish a headquarters amidst an appropriately wildflower-filled setting.

Since 1965, the New England Wild Flower Society has painstakingly maintained the garden, always remaining loyal to Curtis's dream, but also expanding on his vision. To nurture endangered wildflowers from diverse climates, special habitats have been composed. Beneath woodland groves, hundreds of different shade-loving forest flowers blissfully blossom. From swampy bogs, ferns unfold

their lacy fiddleheads. Alpines nestle between the sun-kissed stones of craggy rock gardens, and prairie bloomers frolic with vivid sheen across a rustling, wind-strewn meadow.

The path that penetrates deep into Garden in the Woods begins its journey slowly at a sparsely planted clearing, but then the garden takes flight. It gains momentum gradually with a few choice wildflowers: pink lady's slipper *(Cypripedium acaule)*, white trillium, and bloodroot *(Sanguinaria canadensis)* are scattered sparingly among the leaves. Trees are pruned to hold their crowns high, allowing sun rays to filter through and nourish the creeping phlox *(Phlox stolonifera)*, wood betony *(Pedicularis canadensis)*, and false rue *(Isopyrum biternatum)* that scamper over the ground. At first, the plantings hesitate; there are gaps between the wildflowers. But then, as the trail disappears into the woods, the garden bursts into an unabashed jubilation of color. Everywhere wildflowers are scattered on the forest floor, nestling against shrubs and trees. Endangered species whose numbers are dwindling precariously in the wild find a haven here. Protected from harm, their every whim foreseen and furnished, they run rampant among the oak leaves, rubbing shoulders with one another. Habitats are hewn to accommodate different needs. Bog plants such as the endangered carnivorous pitcher plants *(Sarracenia oreophila)* sink their toes in cool, moist muck, while drought-loving species such as Cumberland rosemary *(Conradina verticillata)* bask on a bed of sun-baked stones.

Trails ramble for two miles or more, deep into the woods, becoming lost in the verdure. Along the way treasures are hidden among the trees. At one point the path descends down steep steps amidst a cloud of whisper-hued, pastel-pink *Rhododendron vaseyi,* while *Magnolia tripetala* spreads immense, umbrellalike leaves in a canopy overhead. In spring, just as the rhododendrons are veiled in color, the magnolia unfolds its oversized, glowing-white blossoms, catching the sun rays two stories up. All the while, below the ivory magnolia, beneath the shell-colored rhododendrons, native ferns—maidenhairs *(Adiantum pedatum)* and Goldie's fern *(Dryopteris goldiana)*—interlace their fronds.

Paths fork and fork again. A high road weaves through glossy beds of wild ginger *(Asarum europaeum)* and the tiny, deep green leaves of dainty *Hosta decorata* 'Thomas Hogg.' Another arm, the low road, descends into a sea of wake-robin *(Trillium viride* var. *luteum)* and red baneberry *(Actaea rubra),* accented by the silver-edged leaves of variegated pachysandra *(Pachysandra terminalis* 'Variegata'). A blanket of oak leaves nestles around the crowns of such albino flowers as white bleeding heart *(Dicentra spectabilis* 'Alba'), while neighboring bushes shoulder sweeping winds.

The path takes a leisurely route to a waterlily pond and then wanders around exploring its shores. May is the most dramatic moment at the pond. Then, a hillside of muted, pastel rhododendrons admiring

Running lickity-split through a clearing, Quaker ladies— also known as bluets—carpet the forest floor with hundreds of tiny blossoms.

Throughout the year, the evergreen Christmas fern (Polystichum acrostichoides) *nestles beside a set of stone steps.*

their reflections in the water forms diffuse puffs of color framing the scene. The glowing amber blooms of *Rhododendron gandavense* × *narcissiflora* spread to interlock fingers with the smoldering pink petals of *Rhododendron catawbiense.* Less dramatic bushes crouch beneath: witch alder *(Fothergilla gardenii),* lowbush blueberry *(Vaccinium angustifolium),* and cushion-soft heathers *(Erica carnea* cultivars) sink their toes into the hillside's well-drained, acid soil, while a network of squat box huckleberries *(Gaylussacia brachycera)* keep the banking from slipping into the waiting waters of the pond below.

Tall, gaudy rose mallows *(Hibiscus moscheutos)* shoot up fast and blossom freely closer to the pond's

A rustic bridge crosses Hop Brook, an ever-flowing stream rushing through the depths of the Garden in the Woods.

By midsummer, the wildflower meadow is ablaze with color. Spires of false indigo (Baptisia australis) *contrast with bright salmon coneflowers.*

Throughout spring, a succession of rhododendrons and azaleas open clouds of blossoms. Rhododendron yedoense var. poukhanense *is an early June attraction.*

Not far into the woods is a sunny banking that creeping phlox (Phlox stolonifera) *has claimed as its own.*

The bird-foot violet (Viola pedata) *winks with royal purple and white-eyed enthusiasm.*

banks, where they can drink to their hearts' content, their toes almost touching the lily-pad-strewn waters. Grasses also stand stately around the water. Zebra grass *(Miscanthus sinensis 'Zebrinus')* holds its feathery white plumes above all, swaying slowly over the more diminutive blades of switch grass *(Panicum virgatum)*. Sun rays fall on the quiet pond, nurturing blossoms nearby. A flock of thirsty flowers, predominately the false dragonhead *(Physostegia virginiana)*, the cardinal flower *(Lobelia cardinalis)*, and the dramatic Turk's-cap lily *(Lilium superbum)*, basks in the sunny setting.

From the lily pond, the path climbs into a laurel bend where native kalmias and other drought-tolerant bushes spread their leathery leaves and blossom where the soil is quenched only with frugal rains. The trail wanders past sunny rock gardens holding their bounty of tiny alpines and into a bog where pitcher plants and cranberries wade amidst fluffy tufts of sphagnum moss. A specially simulated pine barren, crafted to imitate the sterile, acidic soil of the New Jersey shore, skirts both sides of the path. One side holds dry species—poverty grass *(Corema conradii)*, turkeybeard *(Xerophyllum*

Standing stately not far from the water lily pond, Siberian iris (Iris sibirica 'Summer Skies') blossoms in late spring.

asphodeloides), and sand myrtle *(Leiophyllum buxifolium)*. On the opposite side of the path, plants that prefer a moist habitat reside. Staggerbush *(Lyonia mariana)*, cranberries *(Vaccinium macrocarpon)*, and rosettes of the extremely endangered swamp pink *(Helonias bullata)* all sink roots into the specially prepared, lean, peaty soil.

A wildflower meadow stretches not far away. There, black-eyed Susans, asters, blazing star, goldenrod, purple coneflowers, baptisia, and bee-balm form a lush carpet of blossoms. To establish the meadow rapidly, flowering plants were set out at three-foot intervals, and, at the same time, grasses were seeded in. Every fall the meadow is mowed to keep woody plants from encroaching. In midsummer, the path wades through waves of spires and dancing flower heads.

The path roams on, crossing Hop Brook, with its rushing waters gurgling and giggling over rocks in its way, and then twists and turns further into the forest, pausing here and there to peer into a ravine or sweep the edge of a vernal pond. Finally, the path emerges again where it first began, swerving slightly to visit the wildflower nursery.

A Profusion of Violets

A basket brims with Viola odorata rosea *amongst heart-shaped leaves.*

Half buried beneath the snow, a hundred heart-shaped leaves wait for spring. They slumber quietly until one warm, sunny afternoon when the sun awakens their hidden treasures with its strengthening rays. From that moment on, there is no stopping them. Suddenly, the ground is carpeted with flowers.

There is no taming violets. Yet they are endearing and diminutive renegades. Like daffodils, tulips, and grape hyacinths, violets are stars among spring's bounty.

There is no shortage of variety among violets. Popping up wherever they dare, common cultivars such as purple 'Royal Robe', snowy 'White Czar', and blushing pink 'Rosina' are best kept away from prim garden beds.

Bred for vigor, those new hybrids have plenty of gumption but no smell at all, and a violet's scent is its most precious virtue.

Not quite so fleet of foot, the true, fragrant violets—*Viola odorata* and *Viola odorata rosea*—add another element to spring, infusing the season with a scent second to none. Words cannot describe it, other attars can scarcely match it, and, once sampled, that heavenly fragrance is never forgotten. Usually, a violet's unique aroma is only discovered on hands and knees while weeding a bed or plucking a nosegay. But for a few rare moments in spring when the violet bed is sun-kissed and profuse, the perfume floats skyward.

Alas, it is a fleeting pleasure. Violets do not last forever. As soon as summer nights turn balmy and temperatures rise, violets stubbornly refuse to produce buds. Sheltering those sly flowers under shade prolongs the pleasure a few additional weeks. But violets are essentially a spring affair—ethereal and intoxicating.

The pert and fragrant blossoms of Viola odorata *are a spring carpet.*

Very rare, the double blossoms of parma violets are <u>intensely</u> fragrant. Here, tender purple 'Marie Louise' is tucked beside 'Swanley White' and Viola odorata rosea.

Cranbrook's gardens descend a steep hill, skirting the English mansion, above. Inside, all is warm and intimate.

Outside, the grounds are sunswept and radiant. The gardens all focus on sculpture and artifacts, opposite.

This travertine urn is one of a pair brought from Europe by George Booth.

The sky is rich in shimmering sheen
Of deep, delicious blue;
The earth is freshly, softly green,
Of one translucent hue.

Elaine Goodale

RESTORED BY FAITHFUL FRIENDS
THE GARDENS AT CRANBROOK HOUSE

The gardens at Cranbrook were designed as points of departure. They frame the stone, bronze, and marble artwork that they hold; they punctuate and reveal the surrounding Michigan scenery; and they clarify the thoughts of those who come for solace. The gardens are not private, but they are very personal. They hold you momentarily. Then, they send you on.

Cranbrook House was originally the country estate of George Booth, the publisher of *The Detroit News*. Completed in 1908, the red brick English mansion was built as an escape from the bustle of urban life, and as the full time residence of the Booth family. From then on, George, the proud owner of one of the world's first automobiles, motored daily into Detroit at the breakneck speed of three miles per hour.

George Booth came to this country from Canada, and he was continually captivated by the glorious natural landscape of Michigan. He wanted that beauty to be revealed and enhanced in the acreage around his home. Faithful to the fashion of the times,

Cranbrook House sits stately on the crest of a hill, surveying the surrounding scenery. Gradually, the Booths developed a picturesque landscape park skirting and leading up to the Tudor house.

At Cranbrook, pairs and trios of trees—silver maples, redbuds, ginkgos, pines, and tulip poplars—promenade grandly across the lawns adjacent to a circular, climbing drive. The trees are mature now, and their swaying branches stretch leafy fingers up to the clear blue Michigan sky. A sense of security rules this arboreal realm. The trees cradle the visitor in a leafy bower. Then, they step aside to disclose breathtaking vistas ahead or to reveal the sparkling waters of Kingswood Lake below.

With time, formal gardens were added. George Booth had a keen interest in art and often traveled to Europe in pursuit of classical inspiration, returning home laden with sculpted souvenirs from his journeys. Cranbrook's formal gardens were born from the need to frame an incredibly rich and expanding collection of magnificent sculptures and fountains. Three hundred skillfully executed artifacts now reside in the Cranbrook Gardens. Each one is a masterpiece of craftsmanship, and each is surrounded by a setting befitting its grandeur.

While their gardens expanded, the Booths were drawing a circle of talented artistic friends. Gradually, the couple began to formulate a dream. In the 1920s, the first seeds were sown for the creation of an educational community, a place where students could learn amidst an atmosphere interweaving nature, art, and science. The idea grew, nurtured by

Stately delphiniums and peonies stand against the sunken garden wall, where they will not obscure any view.

*Once a vegetable patch, the sunken garden features a center mosaic
composed of annuals surrounded by a very British perennial border.*

the Booths and many other kindred spirits. Today, the grounds are the home of Cranbrook School, Cranbrook Academy of Art, and Cranbrook Institute of Science.

Cranbrook House and its surrounding 40 acres of grounds always remained separate and distinct from the 315 acre Cranbrook campuses. While the campuses merged into modern themes, Cranbrook House remained classical, locked in time.

The glorious Michigan estate flourished until 1949, when the Booths passed away, leaving the Cranbrook campuses well endowed but providing no funds for the upkeep of the gardens. For twenty years, those once magnificent grounds lay totally neglected. Then in 1971, several local garden clubs combined to form an auxiliary to restore and tend the grounds. A legion of volunteers worked tirelessly to return the gardens to their former glory. Now Cranbrook enjoys the services of more than five hundred volunteers who donate a total of seventeen thousand hours yearly to lovingly tend the estate. Now each garden has its own volunteer gardener who labors three days a week planting, grooming, weeding, and replanting. Other volunteers raise funds, lead tours, and work in the greenhouses raising exotic houseplants for their next plant sale.

There is nothing haphazard about Cranbrook. The gardens flow out from the house, descending down the hill in gradual plateaus to the lake below. The formal gardens sink their roots in Italianate themes. Everywhere you wander, the layout, with its strong central axis, whispers of classical roots. The Italian influence is reaffirmed in the bilateral symmetry that prevails. That simple rhythm provides the

The wooded grounds frame the majesty of Kingswood Lake, above. From July onward, hemerocallis flowers, opposite, top, only to wither before nightfall. Lilies stand against the sunken garden wall, basking in the sun, opposite, below.

balance necessary to frame fountains and sculpture softly, without distraction.

The plants also play their role as stewards of sculpture. The soft blues, pinks, and yellows that compose the plantings never draw attention to themselves. Instead, the plants modestly send the visitor's eye to the visage of a god, goddess, or mythological beast cavorting somewhere close by. The statuary, in turn, directs one's gaze to some distant vista carved out of the magnificent Michigan landscape. All is portrayed with mutual admiration—the gardens frame nature in its broadest sense.

At Cranbrook, art and nature are displayed hand in hand, revealed in all their many nuances. The most spectacular and carefully orchestrated sequence of vistas is presented with a grand flourish from the terraces behind Cranbrook House. A grassy promenade runs parallel to the house, disclosing the same view that the Booths admired from the picture windows of their mansion's library. Two British lead statues usher the visitor onward. Surrounded by a grove of four gigantic standard-form bay trees, *Laurus nobilis*, a young British gardener stands ready for work, proudly wielding his poised shovel. A matching grove of bays waits not far away, encircling the gardener's lass, who is offering a basket of freshly harvested apples. Eighteen immense bay standards are sprinkled throughout the Cranbrook grounds, and each must be carted into a cool storage garage before winter; those tender Mediterranean natives would never withstand the Michigan frosts.

A garden flows along the balustrade, framing the view from the crystal windows of the mansion. This is Ellen's Garden, named in honor of George's wife

and still planted faithfully with combinations of her favorite color scheme: lush lavenders, pinks, and silvers perform without pause throughout the seasons. In spring, forget-me-nots, columbine, and *Allium aflatunense*, with its three-foot-tall stems bearing colorful drumsticks, provide shades of lavender and pink, while *Veronica incana* and *Artemisia* 'Silver King' spread a soft bed of silver. Later, the lavender theme is kept alive by still taller globes of *Allium giganteum* standing head and shoulders above bearded iris, *Salvia × superba*, and *Clematis integrifolia* (a bush-type species crowned by nodding blue flowers). By the time July arrives, those perennials are joined by a much shorter flowering onion, *Allium senescens*. In autumn, *Platycodon grandiflorus* (the sky blue balloon flower) and liatris have chimed in. When needed, annuals such as pink and lavender petunias, *Salvia farinacea*, heliotrope, and ageratum are plugged in for fillers.

Behind Ellen's garden, the rose-bowered upper balustrade follows the crest of the ridge, parting only in the center where a pair of ferocious travertine lions politely point to the spectacular vista ahead. Directed by their menacing paws, one's gaze is sent both outward and downward. Only then, standing between the lions, is the immensity of the view finally revealed. Below lies a rectangular reflecting pool, lined on either side by sumptuous perennials. The terrain swoops and then climbs, yet the arrow-straight axis is never abandoned. Ahead, along the same line as the reflecting pool, a swath is shorn from the woods to direct one's vision to its crest, where a huge Chinese dog stands silhouetted against the sky. Hidden from view, on the other side of that hill, stands the Cranbrook Art Academy.

The garden waits for such moments. The reflecting pool provides the perfect medium to nurture

Rosa 'Bonica' leans on a balustrade over the reflecting pool.

imagination. At one end, a stone statue of "Harmony" holds her lyre poised in mid-stroke, completely overtaken with the scene unfolding before her. At the other end, a fountain of frolicking sea nymphs plays its unceasing water music. Between, the blue water holds a few solitary waterlilies floating listlessly in the still water. The accompanying perennials that run along the edge add a touch of cultivation contrasted with the surrounding wooded grounds.

Again, the beds act as a frame. They never shriek for attention; their shades are subdued. The hues play variations on the lavender and pink themes of Ellen's Garden. Meant to be viewed from above, the reflecting pool garden takes an impressionistic approach to produce its effect. The beds are divided nearly into thirds with yellow and blue combinations commanding each end, balanced by white in the center. But, with true artistic dexterity, each section allows a scattering of sympathetic colors to embroider on the prevailing motif. White flowering plants slip here and there into the blue sections to soften the transition. Yellow bloomers occasionally infiltrate the white beds. And green is the underlying base, picking up on the sparkling water's hues.

Each bed is immaculately manicured. As soon as a perennial finishes its display, the blossom heads are immediately whisked away. Good housekeeping maintains a fastidious effect, and it also encourages a second coming for many of the perennials. When their energy is not spent on forming seed heads, the perennials send strength into growth. Often, they oblige with a late season performance accompanied by the chill of the autumn air.

To maintain discipline in those close quarters, some of the more invasive perennials such as yarrow, lamb's ears, and lamium are dug annually, their roots are given a brisk shaking out, and they are

The aquamarine pool accents the central axis of the Cranbrook Italianate design and sends one's eyes roaming up the hill to a path cut from the forest. On the other side of the hill lies Cranbrook Academy of Art.

Close to the bog garden, cosmos, helianthus, and blazing star (Liatris pycnostachya) *combine for an artistic medley of color, texture, and form.*

"Harmony," frozen in continual musical rapture, was carved of stone specifically for this garden by Marco Korbel, the resident Cranbrook sculptor.

replanted in their former spot. The disruption prevents those roamers from proceeding with their usual botanical bullishness. The perennials remain controllable, and they hold a more demure stature. Where plants are used to frame far-off vistas, compactness is preferable.

From the reflecting pool, the gardens continue around the house, with stairways leading from one level to the next. This is a garden of many hills, so the steps are judiciously apportioned in even numbers—easier on ascending feet—and they are served up sparingly. Everywhere, the steps pause at landings so the climber may stop, inhale Michigan air, and enjoy the scenery.

The garden carefully conceals, and then reveals, those distant views. And they too must be maintained. Years ago, George Booth predicted, "Some day, you will garden at Cranbrook with axes instead of hoes." That time has come. Gardeners are continually shearing limbs to open a view in danger of disappearing. The lush scenery forever lies perilously on the verge of being overtaken and overgrown.

Radiating from the house, each garden takes its theme from an incumbent statue or fountain, while the plants all return to the leitmotif of lavenders and yellows first introduced at the reflecting pool. In one garden, a sundial with a ginkgo-leaf-shaped gnomon wades in a sea of blue monkshood, *Salvia farinacea*, and caryopteris. In an herb garden not far away, soft, puffy plants of intricately textured silver and blue herbs billow from triangular beds surrounding a central diamond. Leading the way into the herb garden kneels the likeness of Ecolo, goddess of the earth. This sensitive statue catches the goddess frozen in time, forever donning a pair of sandals to tread the earth softly and protect nature from man's carelessness.

Man's carelessness has taken its toll even in this quiet kingdom. When the auxiliary forged their campaign to reclaim the gardens, they found many of the artifacts damaged by pollution. Most dramatically, the estate's marble pieces were crying for attention. The marble cherubs dancing around a wellhead gracing one exposed overlook had turned from glistening white to pitch black with time, and their tiny toes and flowery garlands had been nibbled away by the elements. In 1980, the auxiliary began a massive restoration project. All the marble statues were buried underneath thick mud packs to soak up impurities. When the mud packs were removed three weeks later, the marble statues underneath glistened sparkling white again. Terracotta was refreshed in whirlpools of hot water to free the clay from fertilizer salts, while bronze statues were sent to experts for professional cleaning. Now the sculptures have all returned home, standing proudly in shimmering shades, almost, but not fully, restored to their former glory. Unfortunately, a

At the other end of the reflecting pool from Harmony stands this three-shelled fountain, purchased in Cannes.

safe method of protecting the fragile stone from the pelting of corrosive rain has yet to be found.

The landscape at Cranbrook is continually evolving, and improvements never pause. Recently, a walled sunken garden was converted from a vegetable patch into a riotously bright annual garden. A ribbon border bursting with a mosaic of color runs pell-mell down the middle. In spring, solid blocks of tulips form a giggling color line down the central walkway. Then, as soon as they bow out, annuals are immediately slipped in to resume the festivities. The colors are vivid and electrifying. These beds take a daring departure and venture into all shades of the rainbow. For the first time at Cranbrook, raucous red is permitted to mingle with more demure blues and pinks.

To subdue the startling effect, softer colors skirt the scene. Nestled against the stone wall that surrounds the garden, a very British perennial bed grows tall and proud. With no view to obscure, delphinium, larkspur, hollyhock, and phlox can stretch their spires. Without color constrictions, pastel hemerocallis, striking red centrathrus, and glowing *Aster* 'Alma Potschke' can all coexist in typical British off-handed disarray. Against their warm brick wall, they expand amidst a backdrop of Boston ivy *(Parthenocissus tricuspidata)*. In a far corner, Siberian gooseberry *(Actinidia arguta)* struggles to set fruit. And clematis, planted to camouflage water pipes, scrambles to grab a foothold.

Cranbrook is not all staid and solemn; it has its lighter moments as well. Not far from the cupids dancing around the wellhead, a bronze and marble statue depicts four young rowdies throwing turtles into a fountainhead. Elsewhere, hidden in a quiet glade of evergreens, a water folly awaits the unsuspecting visitor. When the uninitiated approach to admire a stern bust of Zeus, their footfall on a certain paving stone sends a stream of water jutting from the statue's eyes. Startled, they naturally step away, and a final trickle of water runs down Zeus's

A revelry of mischievous youths cavort around the base of the Wellwishers' Well, recently restored by the Cranbrook auxiliary.

cheek—the statue weeps.

Surprises unfold even for those who know Cranbrook intimately. Not many years ago, a volunteer discovered a set of stepping stones disappearing into the woods. She followed the path, fighting her way through a swamp overgrown with staghorn sumac and raspberry brambles to find a forgotten treasure. There lay the skeleton of a bog garden. With a great deal of digging and mucking, the garden was replanted and now provides an early primrose display accompanied by the gentle aroma of five thousand lily-of-the-valley blossoms all opening in fragrant unison. Fiddleheads sprout in spring followed by lady's slippers, jack-in-the-pulpit, violets, trilliums, fringed gentian, and hepaticas.

Such finds are rare treasures, so the delight was doubled when a similar discovery was made the following year. This time, a gardener's retriever bounded into the brush near the lake. Diving into the brush in hot pursuit, the gardener found her puppy playing in a clearing amidst the pagodas and bridges of a deserted Oriental garden.

Now, the newly restored Oriental garden provides

In front of a lavender backdrop, Petunia 'Azure Pearl' strikes stunning shades of purple that fade with time but never appear insipid.

The Lily Pond at Cranbrook

Framing the view from the library of Cranbrook House, Ellen's Garden,
named for Mrs. Ellen Scripps Booth, overlooks the reflecting pool.

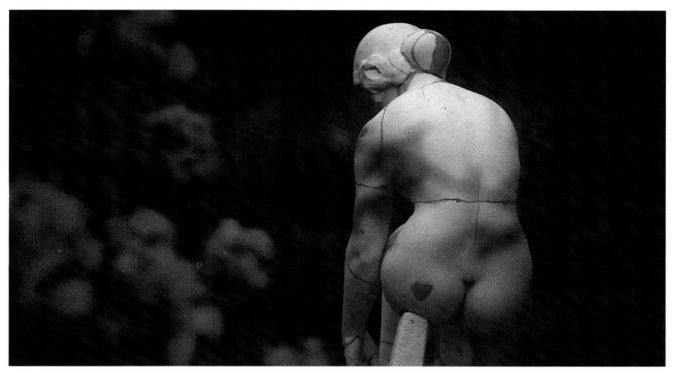

Leading into the herb garden, Ecolo, the goddess of earth,
laces her sandals to walk softly with nature.

the perfect departure from the straight, severe lines of the Italian gardens that predominate on the grounds. Its curvaceous paths meander around a pond edged with the gigantic spreading foliage of petasites and hosta mixed with the more demure dappled leaves of pulmonaria. The arboreal dimensions are also delightfully different from those elsewhere on the estate. Trained to assume a stooped rather than a straight posture, skillfully dwarfed bald cypresses, camperdown elms, tamaracks, redbuds, and crabapples crouch at the pond's edge, their cramped toes nearly touching the water.

Hidden in its thicket, the Oriental garden has music of its own. A sluiceway sends water rushing and roaring into its pond and forces the flow around a tiny island. Informal benches made of lashed tree branches wait for visitors who might wander in to contemplate the secret scene wrapped by verdure. Like all the gardens at Cranbrook, the Oriental garden feeds quiet thoughts.

The Cranbrook gardens are all quiet enclaves, serene spots where only the sounds of nature are heard. Now and then a visitor slips in to draw insight from earth-born art. Weavers come to watch the ever-changing shades of color, sculptors to see the multitude of forms. The gardens inspire all who enter. They hold their visitors for a minute or more in the tranquillity of their leafy confines and then send them onward, strengthened by the insight, to explore further vistas.

A Garden of Old Masters

Beside a garden gate, a wood nymph lies lost in daydreams. Captive in her temple, a maiden rests in eternal reverie. Pan crouches, his music poised in mid-note. Statues can be placed to set the garden's mood. On their lips rests a silent greeting etched in stone. Puckish or somber, staid or caught in motion, sculpture complements the genius of a place.

Somehow, statues speak most eloquently when tucked in shrubbery or half hidden in verdure. They settle in as the garden's permanent residents; they are the sentinels of the landscape. Visitors, taken by surprise, catch them as they frolic with delightful spontaneity among the flowers. We see only a moment in their lives; the remainder of their days are spent immersed in nature's drama. Somehow, statues always appear to hold the secrets of their botanical bedfellows. Their special knowledge might make us better gardeners if only they would share. But the stone refuses to speak.

Sculpture is the only truly reliable ingredient in a composition of unrelenting flux. Plants come and go, lavenders will perish inexplicably during a turbulent winter, and a foxglove will

Joanna Reed's children once wove flower wreaths to crown this statue, called "Christopher," top. Lost in a daydream, a wood nymph, above, rests near the garden gate.

sprout seemingly from nowhere, but the sculpture standing nearby never bats an eyelash. Yet the seasons do effect the garden's

Pan is caught with his pipes poised to serenade the garden with mischievous melodies.

figures. In spring, a statue stands tall amongst its flock of newly arisen flowers. By midsummer, that same statue seems dwarfed against its backdrop of lush verdure. As flowers open, they enhance a sculpture's patina. Apple blossoms and dogwood make marble and limestone step back into a scene, whereas dark evergreens allow bleached stone to move prominently forward. Deep greens make weathered copper more lustrous.

Sculpture adds another dimension to a scene. A bust on its pedestal or a tall, classical figure wading amidst a field of daffodils suddenly lends height and introduces the sky into the composition. Elsewhere, a squat statue with curved lines anchors a tall planting to the ground. Any sculpture set on a wall—a cupid sprawling on cement or a jardiniere overflowing with flowers—instantly renders that fence less intimidating. Statues standing at the entrance of any scene—even a pair of gargoyles guarding a gate—lend an air of mystery and lure visitors onward.

Time plays lightly with sculpture but does not overlook it altogether. Terra-cotta will crack in cold, wet weather. Pots should be emptied of soil before the first harsh frost and sheltered indoors for the winter. If left to brave the elements outdoors, they should be turned upside down and elevated off the ground on wood slabs. Energetic roots can put pressure on a pot's periphery and cause cracking if not root-pruned regularly. Lead can soften with the heat of the blazing midsummer sun, iron will rust in the rain if left unpainted, and stone should be washed free of contaminants.

In some cases, time's mischief is purposely invited and perhaps even hastened. Mosses might be encouraged to nestle on stone in a shady spot. If the pedestal of a statue is soaked with fertilizer, moss will more swiftly settle in. Lichens can be scraped off the north side of trees and glued on sculpture to multiply. In the garden, there is a certain integrity that comes with age. A vintage piece of statuary bestows a certain esteem on its surroundings.

Sculpture takes a multitude of forms. Stern-faced saints, swooning lovers, cupids giggling capriciously, and goddesses eternally staring into space all find a place in the garden. Stone plaques set in the ground might have wise or enigmatic words inscribed on their glistening surface. Artistic animals—either realistic or surrealistic—may cavort through the scene. Fountains are always welcome, singing their splash of music. Bas-relief imbedded in a wall gives depth and integrity, especially when half hidden by vines. A bird bath, a baptismal font, or an old millstone—all are appropriate. The secret lies in subtlety. Sculpture becomes more splendid when offered sparingly.

The statues in a garden never speak, but they never remain mute, either. Combined with plants, sculpture—whether complex and classical or smooth and modern—complements the many faces of a landscape.

The Wellwisher's Well at Cranbrook

From The Bishop's Garden, this is the view, above, of the Washington National Cathedral and its "shadow house." One of the gardeners has collected a basket of strewing herbs for an upcoming wedding, opposite.

Hope looks out
Into the dazzling sheen, and fondly talks
Of summer . . .

Anonymous

A GARDEN LEGACY REDISCOVERED
THE BISHOP'S GARDEN
AT THE WASHINGTON NATIONAL CATHEDRAL

Night and day, the time-worn wooden doors to the Bishop's Garden always stand ajar. The garden, with its meditative boxwood-entwined walkways leading to ivy-enshrouded benches, waits to embrace all who might seek an introspective moment.

Spread in the shadow of the soaring buttresses supporting the south tower of the majestic Gothic-style National Cathedral, the Bishop's Garden is but one element of the plantings on the cathedral close. Gardens sprout here and there throughout the fifty-seven acres skirting the cathedral spires. Fountains and ivy adorn courtyards tucked between the but-

tresses. Luscious 'Red Illusion' roses lean heavily against old stone retaining walls. A forest composed of white American redbuds *(Cercis canadensis alba)*, white oaks *(Quercus alba)*, red oaks *(Quercus rubra)* and American beech *(Fagus grandifolia)* lines the Pilgrim Road leading to the cathedral doors. Farther from the spires, a wildflower walk meanders moodily through the woods for those who wish to depart deeper into nature.

The cathedral is surrounded by plantings, but a special mood prevails in the monastic Bishop's Garden with its fourteenth-century flavor. Designed in 1925 by Frederick Law Olmstead, Jr., and realized

Shading the shadow house, this thicket of crepe myrtle gives the Bishop's Garden
a lovely burst of color in the spring.

with the help of Florence Bratenahl, wife of the second dean of the cathedral, the Bishop's Garden has roots deep in the past.

A single path leads in from the entryway arch. And, for the first few feet, the narrow boxwood-encased alleyway yields no hint of the fragrant herbs and redolent roses that are bedded only steps away. It is a secret passage, a place that encourages inward thoughts while also holding a promise. The gray stone walk leads onward, rounds a bend, and suddenly reveals the first furtive glimpse of the Bishop's Garden, framed in lush greenery.

The magnificent boxwood hedges accompany the path along its journey throughout the gardens. The boxwood's lacy branches part only to reveal a twelfth-century Norman arch and court, to disclose walls inlaid with bas-reliefs of saints and martyrs dimpled and flecked by the fingers of centuries, or to invite entry into another garden "room."

Most of the small, self-contained rooms are introspective, encouraging visitors to enter and explore within. But the bishop's lawn takes a sweeping view. Opening out like a carpet of sunbeams from the shady Norman court and introduced by twin Atlas cedars (*Cedrus atlantica* 'Glauca') waving their blue-green branches in every breeze, the Bishop's lawn is surrounded on every side by blossom-laden bushes. White and yellow flowers tangle in heavenly profusion. Potentillas, brooms, and hypericums combine their vibrant yellow blossoms with pristine 'White Innocence' peonies, creamy viburnums, and spires of *Buddleia davidii* 'White Bouquet' attracting a flutter of golden swallowtail butterflies. Shading a comfortable garden bench, the golden rain tree *(Koelreuteria paniculata)*, the lawn's focal point, reaches leafy branches skyward. In summer, its deep green leaves are smothered in smoldering yellow blossoms. In autumn, those same branches carry a heavy burden of rust-colored seed pods to match the hues of fallen leaves, stretching like a sea of delicate color underfoot.

After a stroll in the sparkling grass of the Bishop's lawn, a "shadow house" awaits, lined with comfortable, protected benches. Built of stone from President Cleveland's summer residence, the octagonal garden house was designed to echo the cathedral, each of its arched Gothic windows framing a view of the garden. And in spring, the gracefully weeping boughs of the golden chain tree *(Laburnum × watereri* 'Vossii') send showers of glinting, sun-ray blossoms to further enfold the scene.

The shadow house overlooks the *hortulus*, or "little garden," with its authentic Carolingian (751–907 A.D.) planting staged around a gaping white baptismal font originally carved in 835 A.D. Members of the All Hallows Guild, a group of volunteers responsible for maintaining all the gardens on the cathedral close, painstakingly researched medieval literature to find herbs faithful to the period of the sparkling white baptismal font standing in the center of the beds. Only herbs described in Charlemagne's garden list; in *The Plan of St. Gall*, a map of a Benedictine monastic community, dated about 820; or in a poem written in 849 by a Benedictine monk named Walafrid Strabo are permitted in this garden. Garlic, dill, southernwood, feverfew, clary sage, betony, and black cumin mingle their essential oils in the beds. Forming a ring of lace dancing around the font, winter hardy rosemary, *Rosmarinus*

officinalis 'ARP', stands no taller than a foot.

Not far away, the gray stone walk merges into red brick under foot and a rose garden blossoms with a profuse medley of floribundas surrounding a grassy rectangle where sparrows flit. A splash of color greets the eye from the combined hues of 'Crimson Glory', 'Double Delight', 'Fragrant Cloud', 'Ma Perkins', 'Tropicana', and, of course, 'Mister Lincoln', many chosen for their fragrance.

Herbs surrounding an old English sundial—lavender for devotion, sage for wisdom, rosemary for remembrance—are laid in a patchwork bed. Close by, a wayside cross, once a beacon guiding the way for early Christian pilgrims, stands in a bed of flowers, and, medlar *(Mespilus germanica)*, a very rare antique tree famed for its immense, fragrant blossoms followed by apple-like fruit, stretches its mahogany branches.

Against the heat of the south-facing garden wall, a perennial border holds its color until Thanksgiving. Porcelain pink Japanese anemones, *Aster novae-angliae* 'Harrington's Pink', whisper-pink roses, snow-white Nippon daisies, heliopsis, dicentra, and a chorus of other delicately colored blossoms intertwine before a bas-relief of St. Catherine. A fountain slowly trickles into a pool shaped in the form of a primitive cross.

The Bishop's Garden is for exploring. The gray stone walkway meanders, twisting and turning, revealing snippets of gardens and offering the opportunity to explore any alcove more fully. Along the way, benches wait—some shaded in the boughs of trees, others washed in a shaft of sunbeams. Sometimes the walk is submerged in a canopy of evergreens; sometimes it basks in a patch of unfiltered sun rays. Wherever the path roams, it never reveals all its facets at once.

Heritage Herbs

awn slips slowly into the *hortulus*, the "little garden" at Washington National Cathedral. It creeps lightly, running its rays through tufts of leafy herbs. The textures of thyme and savory mingle as lacy fennel *(Foeniculum vulgare)* stretches its leaves skyward. Wild ginger *(Asarum europaeum)* and creeping pennyroyal *(Mentha pulegium)* roam aimlessly around the ankles of grassy chives *(Allium schoenoprasum)*. The morning sun wanders slowly, illuminating each crescent-shaped bed individually until finally the whole garden is aglow.

A quiet beauty resides throughout the *hortulus*. Flowers are rare within its boxwood hedges. Instead, leaves interplay in a kingdom composed of muted greens and lacy silvers. A brush of the hand releases a deliciously heady infusion of aromas. A potpourri of fresh, earthy scents accompanies every footfall.

Like a lush medieval tapestry, crescent-shaped raised beds cluster closely around the time-worn baptismal font. Surround-

A basket is filled with freshly cut rosemary, dill, statice, golden sage, purple sage, tricolor sage, and southernwood.

ing herbs echo the mood of a medieval garden. In the *hortulus*, each plant has an ancient medicinal purpose. The betony *(Stachys officinalis)*, which edges a gray stone pathway, was employed to drive away both devils and despair. Southernwood *(Artemisia abrotanum)* was administered to those that "shake or shudder with colde." Artisans drank rue *(Ruta graveolens)* daily to preserve their sight. Fleur-de-lis *(Iris × germanica* 'Florentina') was used as a fixative, and sage *(Salvia officinalis)* promised longevity.

Although volunteers of the All Hallows Guild carefully searched for vintage herbs when designing the garden, they used some poetic license. Many ancient herbs can be invasive, stepping on the toes of their bedfellows. Rather than inviting roving wormwood *(Artemisia absinthium)* into the snug beds, the gardeners planted the more compact and controllable *Artemisia* 'Powis Castle'. Instead of planting tender rosemary *(Rosmarinus officinalis)* to encircle the baptismal font, they used winter-hardy *Rosmarinus officinalis* 'Arp'. Purple sage *(Salvia officinalis* 'Purpurea') substitutes for the green species, adding a dash of color.

Harmony pervades the contemplative *hortulus*. Minutes slip by, marked on the ancient sundial, while soft, feathery herbs bend and stretch, begging to be touched. Within the boxwood hedge that borders the little garden, a dozen scents mingle to compose an ever-changing potpourri. A nearby bench waits for anyone to sit and enjoy the nectar of herbs steeped in history.

A shadow house overlooks the tapestry of herbs in Washington Cathedral's medieval garden, as a nearby sundial marks the fleeting hours.

A Moment of Peace at the Bishop's Garden

Hummingbirds sip from lush peach 'Bridesmaid' azaleas billowing over neatly clipped English boxwood hedges. Wing Haven boasts ten dripping bird baths like that shown opposite.

All ye who humbly enter here
Are welcome and to Wing Haven dear,
Behold earth's beauty, the heavens above,
Yet if some presence other than doves
Should startle you,
Fear not . . . for tis God!

Paul Carpenter, Jr.

A GENTLE REFUGE

WING HAVEN

lizabeth and Edwin Clarkson were sitting side by side on a crescent-shaped cement bench contemplating the surrounding flutterings and warblings when they decided to name their garden Wing Haven. Ever since, this 3½-acre landscape not far from the center of Charlotte, North Carolina, has truly been a haven for feathered visitors of all types. The Clarksons recorded over 140 different species coming and going, wooing and nesting in the trees, arbors, and hedges around Wing Haven. In addition to the permanent population of cardinals, chickadees, wrens, warblers, titmice, and dozens of other birds, the Clarksons have attracted such rarities as golden-crowned kinglets, American kestrels, Eastern bluebirds, and little blue herons. Twice bald eagles were seen paying January visits to Wing Haven. Even the shy whippoorwill's lonesome note has been heard echoing from the shadows of Wing Haven's woods.

Throughout their courtship, Edwin and Elizabeth had exchanged long letters about their dream house being built in Charlotte. Edwin waxed eloquent describing the terrace he had built and the arrow-straight willow oak in the yard. However, he

One View of the Landscape at Wing Haven

neglected to mention that the willow oak was the only tree on the property. When Elizabeth arrived at her new home in mid April of 1927, she stood on the newly built terrace staring at a completely barren landscape with nothing but Carolina red clay as far as the eye could see. She immediately set to work amending the soil—digging out beds and mixing the clay with peat, compost, sand, and topsoil. Then, she hurriedly slipped in some marigolds around the house to tide her through that first bleak season.

Initially, the Clarksons had no real vision for their garden other than a burning desire to be surrounded by lush greenery. Their plan was simply to create a neatly hedged formal landscape where they might wander after dinner on an evening walk. The garden evolved with prim boxwood borders shepherding billowing azaleas overburdened by pastel blossoms. Overhead, a canopy of paler pink double and single flowering cherries bowered the paths in lacy branches.

Not long after the Clarksons were married, Elizabeth became ill with Malta fever and—of necessity—began to spend warm afternoons resting on the brick terrace. It was then that she befriended the birds. As she sat very still, winged friends began to alight on her outstretched finger. Before long, she was feeding them from her hand—a feat few birdwatchers have successfully accomplished. From that moment on, the gardens had a purpose: They were devoted to attracting birds.

At Wing Haven, the entire garden is tucked within a six-foot pierced brick wall to protect its feathered residents from prowling neighborhood pets. Safe from harm, the birds flit through holly hedges and settle on the branches of dogwood trees. They forage on the fruit of mulberry, pokeberry,

elderberry, and chokecherry bushes and steal purple clusters of Muscadine grapes. They find solace regardless of the season. Throughout fall and early winter, an arbor of Russian olive *(Elaeagnus angustifolia)* offers a banquet of berries, while huge hedges of evergreen Amur River privet *(Ligustrum amurense)* provide shelter and hold fruit in the bleakest months.

In early spring, a gateway trellis interwoven with *Clematis armandii* is busy with the activity of nest building. A few brief weeks later, the nest disappears into a cloud of white blossoms that send their vanilla-sweet scent floating whenever fluttering wings enter the floral tangle. Still later in summer, that same clematis will donate its downy seedpods to feather another bird's nest.

At Wing Haven, everything is orchestrated for the birds. Fragrant pink azaleas, such as the rose-throated 'George A. Taber', peachy 'Coral Bells', and scarlet-hued torch azalea 'Kaempferi', are overburdened with nectar-bearing blooms for darting hummingbirds. Later in the season the thimble-sized hummingbirds sip from the cardinal flower *(Lobelia cardinalis)*, crape myrtle *(Lagerstroemia indica)*, impatiens, trumpet vine *(Campsis radi-*

Perched above the garden, a yellow-rumped warbler whistles his sleigh-bell trill.

Every pathway ends in a view. This path leads under a wisteria arbor designed to attract nesting birds in spring.

cans) and honeysuckle snags. Birds splash in bird baths that remain heated in winter. Shallow pools—never deeper than two inches—provide places where feathered visitors can frolic. In the man-made woods that now border the garden, weathered stumps are left standing for woodpeckers. Chemicals of any sort—including chemical fertilizers—are prohibited to save the birds from poisons.

Wildlife reigns at Wing Haven, but the gardens are anything but haphazard. Every path boasts a carefully composed view. In the formal sections of the garden, brick paths march sternly through tunnels of lush azaleas and rose-embowered arch-ways. Immaculately painted, pure white cast-iron garden chairs and benches sit waiting for guests to rest quietly while watching the swoopings and chirpings of birds. A neatly filigreed sectional seat surrounds the original willow oak, now ninety feet tall.

But not all the walkways are meant for human visitors. Visitors are not allowed to tread on grassy areas between brick paths, lest they disturb busy robins searching for worms. Even the Clarksons took the winding path around the periphery of their garden rather than promenade through the middle. The wooded periphery path has surprises of its own as it meanders past a wildflower-filled frog hollow and

Brick paths are everywhere at Wing Haven. The Clarksons gave each other gifts of bricks for anniversaries and birthdays until they had 350,000—enough to build ten houses.

through a thicket of honeysuckle. Once in a while, the trail swerves toward the formal garden to reveal a glimpse of vista dominated by azaleas.

Although Wing Haven is a small garden, it boasts a diversity of spaces. Surrounding a sundial is an aromatic herb garden divided into four quadrants holding culinary herbs, fragrant herbs, medicinal herbs, and Biblical herbs in beds edged with Korean boxwood *(Buxus microphylla koreana)*. Not far away, English boxwood encases a bed of intoxicatingly fragrant blue violets *(Viola odorata)*. Behind the house, a broad, grassy lawn encased in Amur River privet is edged with white pansies in spring, followed by clouds of pink impatiens in summer. A rose garden that once held three hun-

dred different varieties is now composed only of the hardiest types that will survive without chemical applications to prevent disease and dispatch pests. Six-foot-tall pillars of the whisper-pink grandiflora 'Queen Elizabeth' stand beside 'Pink Radiance,' a glowing hybrid tea. Not far away, a lush arbor of 'Frau Karl Druschki', transplanted from Elizabeth's childhood home in Texas, forms a snowflake-white garland overhead.

A patio overlooks the garden. Every evening, Elizabeth and Edwin dined under a wooden pergola overlooking their cherry blossom strewn paths. The birds became accustomed to their company, and later, when Elizabeth wandered through the garden carrying her little pink tin filled with fresh beetle

Throughout Wing Haven, plaques are embedded in the brick. A special verse was composed for the entry gates of the garden.

One evening, sitting side by side on this crescent-shaped bench, the Clarksons decided to name their garden Wing Haven.

grubs and mealworms, wrens would alight on her finger begging to be fed. Orphaned bluebirds grew up in her library roosting on *Roget's Thesaurus*, and one spring a family of wrens found a hole in the house and was allowed to take up residence in the guest room. There was Irving, a female wood duck adopted by the Clarksons, and Daphne, a pet rabbit, who sat on Elizabeth's lap. All came of their own accord to live and were raised—free and yet tame—at Wing Haven.

When Elizabeth became ill in 1988, birds flew through her open window to land gently on her deathbed. She passed away peacefully in the knowledge that her garden would go on—for in 1970 the Clarksons had established the Wing Haven Foundation to ensure that the garden would always continue to bloom. Now, the catbirds still come to the outstretched hand of Wing Haven's curator and the Clarksons' gentle treatment of birds continues to this day. *Ah this is glorious news!*

Beauty on the Wing

utterflies perform a winged ballet. Dancing to the rays of the midsummer sun, they endow a garden with extra layers of vibrant color. Below, flower heads calm the tempo, swaying lazily in the breezes. Above, blue sky is shattered by a mad fluttering of wings. When a swarm of butterflies is in motion, all a garden's colors are tossed topsy-turvy into the sky like handfuls of heavenly confetti. For some, butterflies are the capper to any garden—the magnificent made sublime.

A lone butterfly poised on a blossom is a poignant soliloquy; a horde of fluttering *Lepidoptera* is a singularly joyous sight. It is the sort of merriment that rewards gardeners who spread a nectar feast for swallowtails and sulfurs. It is revelry that inspires us to leave the buddleia unpruned and let the parsley blossom to produce the abundance necessary to feed that skylarking band.

Butterflies are sun-worshipping creatures. When warmed by the sun's brilliant rays, their wings grow restless and giddy, taking flight in sheer excitement. Once airborne, butterflies glide and circle, seeking colorful repast. Above all, they prefer the color purple, followed by yellow, pink, and white. In a meadow, they may light on an aster, goldenrod, coneflower, meadowsweet, Queen Anne's lace, thistle, or Joe Pye weed. When contemplating a cultivated garden, they will often show a preference for cosmos, lantana, beebalm, zinnia, phlox, or nicotiana.

Butterflies look for a place where they might settle and sip. A flat surface is custom crafted for balancing long legs and fanning exquisite wings while probing for nectar. Daisies, sedum, verbena, and sweet william are easy to alight on. Yet spires also attract butterflies, who never pause in their labor. Lilacs, buddleia, loosestrife, and mignonette are all irresistible. Aroma calls them forth, luring them to brave any foothold for refreshment.

The garden's most fragile visitors, butterflies are easily hurt. A stiff breeze will shatter their wings; a sudden downpour will soak the powder that keeps them airborne unless a strategically placed windbreak offers blessed shelter. Deciduous trees, especially willows, elms, ashes, and aspens, provide a resting spot on which to pupate as well as a buffer from summer winds. Puddles and shallow troughs become gathering points where gregarious species socialize and sip.

Every butterfly was once a caterpillar, consuming quantities of roughage to prepare for its next life. Somewhere close at hand, provisions can be made for a butterfly's least glamorous stage, as well. Fruit trees, deciduous trees, clovers, lupines, violets, plantain, and parsley will nourish larvae until it is time to slumber, emerge, and take to the skies.

With a cloud of butterflies hovering above, any field becomes a spectacle of nature as dozens of wings catch sun rays and toss them about. There is something breathtaking about butterflies flitting overhead and roaming amongst their flower beds. Butterflies reflect the ephemeral freedom that is midsummer.

*Sunning itself on a zinnia, a black swallowtail pauses
in flight.*

*Double flowers disappoint famished butterflies, but single
flowers, such as this marigold, appease their appetite.*

A giant white coasts over a field of baby's-breath.

The Eastern tiger swallowtail sips from a coneflower.

A Love Temple, above, overlooks a quiet pond. A stone wall is festooned with wisteria, opposite.

Again I say, again I heard,
The rolling river, the morning bird;—
Beauty through my senses stole;
I yielded myself to the perfect whole.

Ralph Waldo Emerson

THE HEART
OF AMERICAN GARDENING
LONGWOOD GARDENS

When artists seek inspiration, they wander amongst the works of the Old Masters in museums. When gardeners need inspiration, they go to Longwood. There, they can ramble between walkways bowered in verdant lushness or stroll in a sea of flowering color. Longwood nurtures your imagination.

Longwood Gardens, a grand estate near Kennett Square, Pennsylvania, is a massive celebration of botanical beauty. And from their beginning, the gardens were dedicated to nurturing fantasy. As you meander slowly along the brick paths, a series of carefully orchestrated scenes unfold, inspiring memories that linger, later to return again and again.

Longwood is a series of expertly crafted and ever-changing vignettes composed to portray the full glory of nature in all its facets. Magnolias heavy with an abundance of plump pink blossoms stretch their

The airy blossoms of Hydrangea macrophylla *appear to be floating above the foliage.*

Forget-me-nots, Myosotis sylvatica, *form a carpet at the feet of wisteria standards.*

Astilbes proudly sway in spring breezes.

Rhododendrons and azaleas tumble down a hillside.

limbs, forming a wide canopy above a meadow of merry daffodils. In a hushed forest of sparsely planted trees, shafts of sunlight infiltrate and illuminate an ocean of flowering azaleas spilling down a flowing hillside.

Depending upon the season, a multitude of blossoming vines lounge lackadaisically over old brick walls or lean on open pergolas. Throughout spring and summer, the fuzzy-leaved, delectable kiwi vine, *Actinidia chinensis*, gropes its felted branches on a sturdy frame, beckoning visitors to explore onward. As summer waxes, *Hydrangea macrophylla* smothers its deeply textured leaves in a froth of lace cap umbels. In autumn, *Clematis paniculata* completely encases its support in a cloud of intoxicating, spicy white flowers. Longwood is a wonderland of ideas.

Although the gardens are influenced by Italian, French Renaissance, and picturesque English landscapes, there is a thread that weaves throughout the grounds—the plants themselves provide the unity at Longwood. Everywhere he traveled, owner Pierre S. du Pont, an industrial wizard and garden builder *par excellence*, visited the local nurserymen and brought home cuttings or seeds. He imported choice grapevines, figs, oranges, lemons, and limes from nurseries in Britain and California and introduced *Acacia floribunda* and *Acacia leprosa*, two treelike members of the mimosa family, from growers in France. Dozens of azalea hybrids were sent from Belgium to fill a glasshouse devoted entirely to previewing the glowing pastel shades of spring. From Hawaii came hybrid cattleya, phalaenopsis, and dendrobium orchids to display in a set of showcases flanking the conservatory doors. Throughout his lifetime, du Pont amassed an incredible array of diverse and rare plants to fill the gardens of his grand estate. And the botanical collection continues to expand. Truly the center for gardening in America, Longwood has financed plant-finding expeditions to all corners of the globe. At present, the gardens boast 11,000 different types of plants, each featured to shine.

When Pierre du Pont bought the land that he would call Longwood, he already had a vision for planting his estate. With no formal horticultural training but schooled from a copy of Samuel Parsons' classic, *How to Plan the Home Grounds* and aided by his own keen intuition, du Pont conceived his first ambitious project: an old-fashioned, six hundred-foot-long perennial border called the Flower Garden Walk. Such a lengthy walk must offer a goal at journey's end. To fulfill its promise, the leisurely brick promenade leads straight to a round fountain that provides a focal point and refreshes with a spray of chilly water. In the opposite direction, a cozy bench offers a respite for the weary walker.

Along the way, the Flower Garden Walk reveals a sumptuous botanical feast all laid out in an artistically composed spread. Originally, the walk was planted primarily with perennials and biennials to hark back to the cottage gardens so popular in quiet hamlets of Britain. Hollyhocks, lilacs, and snapdragons waded in a sea of roses, peonies, and iris. But, over the years, the capricious perennials were replaced with more reliable annuals that can be lifted and renewed as the season progresses.

In its journey along the entire spectrum of carefully balanced hues, the border begins with pure white beds. Verbenas, cleome, zinnias, candytuft, and pansies line the walkway with snow white shades. Then, the border melts into the hot colors of red, orange, and yellow provided by calendulas, ornamental peppers, cannas, celosia, tulips, and zinnias. A few steps further along the avenue and

A secret Italian water garden is hidden behind a wall of tall linden trees.

those sizzling, fiery hues are relieved by pink stocks and cool red verbenas accented by a shy purple salvia or two. Finally, the border sinks into a refreshing medley of purple and blue lobelia, salvia, viola, and ageratum nestled amongst silver foliage plants. To keep the eye from straying, an arborvitae hedge provides a discrete curtain.

The border never pauses throughout the season. Just as one botanical performer fades, another quickly takes its place. In spring, English daisies (*Bellis*), tulips, and pansies rule the design. In autumn, chrysanthemums and coleus are tucked in where early performers faded. The walk is forever lush and dreamy; and its design sets the stage for the entire estate. That wide, arrow-straight brick path forms the axis from which further gardens radiate and expand on their different themes.

A total of 1050 acres is maintained at Longwood and on many the plantings are an eclectic interpretation of the world's premiere gardens, all fashioned according to the du Pont vision of paradise. Over the years, Pierre designed a secret rose path where the visitor might walk encased under a canopy of scrambling 'American Pillar' roses. He acquired a semicircular whispering bench where companions might sit on opposite corners, share confidences, and catch every word unbeknownst to passersby. He erected a Love Temple where a tryst could be accomplished within a discrete screen of grapevines and no one would be the wiser. He made woodland walks of deeply colored rhododendrons for contemplative strolls.

Friends might stop for a tête-à-tête in a peony garden where sizzling golden Saunders's hybrid tree peonies bear their burden of immense fluffy blossoms complemented by the cooler shades of purple and ice blue Siberian iris. Above these flowers, *Laburnum* × *watereri* 'Vossii' the golden chain tree, simultaneously bursts into showers of sun-shaft yel-

In spring, rhododendrons and azaleas bear their bouquet-like umbels of flowers.

low blossoms. There are introspective interludes in an intimate allée of bald cypress, *Taxodium distichum*, bolting up to touch the sky. All the while, in still another corner of the estate, a fortress tower overlooks a rushing waterfall that drowns conversation in the babbling of its tumbling stream.

The melody of splashing water is heard throughout Longwood—Pierre had a passion for water. Everywhere he went, du Pont noticed the fluid elements of gardens. On his return from a tour of Italy, Pierre built the Open Air Theatre featuring a water curtain inspired by the theatre garden at Villa Gori near Siena.

Later, after visiting Villa Gamberaia, near Florence, a discrete Italian Water Garden was added. Italian artisans created urns, gargoyles, filigree, and other fine architectural work all molded in a common fruit-bowl-and-garland pattern. A matching pair of long, curving steps were laid for water to trip and gush as it descends into a garden where water reigns supreme. Arching jets splash, spigots shoot sky high, fountains overflow into opulent basins below, and everywhere the melody of gurgling water fills the air. Hidden in a knoll of stately linden trees, *Tilia cordata*, and discovered only by ambitious hikers who wander past the azalea-bedded woods, the secret Italian Water Garden remains one of Longwood's most delightful surprises.

The culmination of his study of garden fountains is the Main Fountain Garden. Drawing on his memory of works in Italy, France, and the great World's Fairs, du Pont created an unrivaled fountain display, where ornate sun-washed balustrades lead up broad steps into shady porticoes. The magnificent

At Longwood, the flowers never pause. Mounds of blossoming hydrangeas are accented by clouds of hydrangea baskets overhead.

structures set a backdrop for fountains to play their melodic water music. Plants are not important characters in this scene; the Main Fountain Garden features only a few strategically placed Norway maples, boxwood, agaves, and ivies that create a green backdrop to the water's frenzy.

Not content to merely array the summer months in verdure, du Pont built an immense conservatory choreographed to portray a parklike scene despite the weather outdoors. Protected snugly under a latticework of glass, a serpentine brook meanders amongst banks featuring plantings that change with the season. In February, cyclamens run along the banking, blooming in rich sweetheart red and white hues. In November, chrysanthemums emblazon the banks of the indoor brook. During the Easter holi-

Amid the greenery at Longwood, classic Italian urns set the mood.

A tangle of clematis is ready to bloom on a terrace overlook.

days, whisper pink cymbidium orchids are reflected in the pale blue water.

To keep visitors wandering, the conservatory walkways are lined with colorful bedded flowers. Textures, shades, and forms are all carefully balanced. The color combination might be composed of shocking pink hydrangeas against royal purple nierembergia in the spring or spears of soft lilac *Salvia leucantha* jutting from tufts of frilly white spider chrysanthemums in autumn. No matter which medley is featured, the plantings always slip into variations on that theme. If the beds are a

After an introspective ramble, friends can murmur confidences in the secrecy of a whispering bench sunken into a hornbeam hedge.

rhapsody in pink hydrangeas, then pink hydrangeas appear again sculpted into single-stemmed, rounded-crown standards. If chrysanthemums are being profiled along the walkways, they also fill immense chandelierlike hanging baskets swaying overhead.

In this park under glass, all the workings are hidden from view. Heating elements are sunken below walkways while supporting cement columns are encased in a camouflage of *Ficus pumila*, the creeping fig. Roving vines such as blazing magenta *Bougainvillea* 'Penang', watery blue *Plumbago au riculata*, and the golden trumpets of *Allamanda*

cathartica 'Williamsii', encase entryways, enticing visitors to penetrate further into the jungle. Passageways are embowered with *Acacia leprosa* trained to climb and form a tangle of fluffy yellow blossoms. Gigantic nephrolepis ferns send their croziers spilling from immense baskets overhead. Wandering in the conservatory is like a tropical ramble while the world outdoors is wrapped in midwinter.

All the gardens at Longwood serenade your senses. A quiet alcove might speak of serenity while another planting is busy with a bright yellow, red, and blue combination of spring bulbs. The recessed whispering bench hidden in its clipped hornbeam hedge nurtures solitude while, not far away, the expansive water garden has a social ambiance. Longwood is deliberately composed to depict a myriad of different moods. Although each garden is orchestrated to carry through and consummate its individual intent, Longwood was not designed as a flowing whole. Pierre du Pont described his gardens as departments, just as you might find in a store. Each department explores one type of plant or expresses a single theme. Hedges or walls separate the grounds and divide compartments. Archways in the hedges send the visitor wandering from one verdant room to the next, where an entirely different experience awaits.

So at Longwood every eye can be pleased, every sense will be satiated. Those intimate garden rooms provide the perfect solution to designing a garden of Longwood's magnitude. The hedges separate the sections, but they beckon you to walk onward and explore. And, somehow, the scene never seems disjointed. Nature works with design while the seasons are the stage. In a place where imagination can freely roam, whimsy is counterpoised against serious themes and somehow they all blend harmoniously.

Longwood always invites the viewer to glimpse again. Strolling past a wisteria wall, one glimpses crab apple blossoms in the distance, framed by a

Delicate jungle blossoms mingle with rowdy field flowers.

In less formal garden, flowering crab apple trees wade ankle deep in an ocean of scattered dandelions.

window of wisteria. For a fleeting second, both plants are seen in an entirely different light. Although you have certainly seen wisteria and cherry blossoms before, now they are seen afresh. Longwood is composed of many such moments. A bed of steel-blue iris is contrasted against a white gravel walk and the hue suddenly stands out more vividly than ever before. A flower-laden weeping rosebud cherry, *Prunus subhirtella* 'Pendula', stands out silhouetted against a deep green hedge of Japanese holly, *Ilex crenata* 'Stokesii', and they are both reflected in a rippling pond to double their color impact and expand their shape. Oceans of daffodils never look more brilliant than when they skirt gnarled heirloom orchard trees. Longwood is so

deliciously fleeting. One week earlier . . . one week later and that special combination of color will vanish, another transient elixir will take its place. Longwood is a tribute to nature in all its many facets.

Longwood has always embraced the public. In fact, every garden at Longwood is designed with a massive audience in mind. In recent years, Longwood has been maintained by a board of trustees that remains totally dedicated to cultivating Pierre du Pont's vision. In keeping with his original plan, the grounds continue to evolve. The gardens grow, they flourish, and they sprout brave new combinations. Always exploring, always looking at botany anew, they flow with the mood of the times. Longwood is composed of a million visions.

Wisteria at Longwood

Giant wisteria standards wade on islands of forget-me-nots.

Wisteria Time

In Longwood's calendar of fleeting events, there is a moment in May that is wrapped in wisteria. Greeting visitors on either side of the entry gates, the sultry vines drip from arbors, sending clusters of soft, lilac-tinted blossoms draping languidly down. If you glimpse through windows in the arbor, you might catch a vision of blooming apple blossoms in the distance. All the while, a sweet, heady fragrance infuses the air. It is a delicious initial taste of Longwood's splendor.

The gate is only a hint of further flowers, and the theme is echoed in Longwood's wisteria garden. In a verdant "room" encased by walls of arborvitae, carefully trained, triple-tiered trees of *Wisteria floribunda*, the Japanese wisteria, sway slowly with every gentle breeze. It is an opulent vision, composed of spilling blossoms floating airily above an ocean strewn with forget-me-nots. The colors melt one into the other—green, deep purple, and lilac are all set against a hazy, misty May morning sky. With the help of gardeners, nature paints a poignant impressionistic picture.

Wisteria floribunda was first introduced into this country from Japan as recently as 1862. Throughout the Victorian Era, the vine remained a favorite with gardeners, often planted to embower a front porch with grape-like clusters of intensely aromatic blossoms. In fact, those front porch plantings were so omnipresent that they forged a personality for the plant. Wisteria will forever remain linked with intimacy, confidences shared, and the slow, still lifestyle that suffuses May.

Wisteria floribunda *weeps clusters of pea-shaped blossoms.*

It is the unhurried early summer mood that Longwood strives to capture during those fleeting moments in mid-May. The grounds boast six types of *Wisteria floribunda* draping colorful blossoms from gnarled stems and perfuming the air throughout the gardens. Included on Longwood's grounds are 'Geisha', 'Alba' (a pure white bloomer), 'Longissima', 'Rosea' (with shell pink blossoms), 'Royal Purple', and 'Violacea Plena' (a double flowering variety). The wisteria garden focuses on two varieties—the lilac colored species *Wisteria floribunda* and the snow white *Wisteria floribunda* 'Alba'.

Planted in 1976, the wisteria garden came to Longwood after Pierre du Pont's lifetime, added to fill the spot that once harbored a quaint period rose garden. The garden is young. And yet, the planting feels as if it has always belonged, due to the retrospective design composed by Thomas Church, a landscape architect famed for his synthesis of Baroque and modern elements.

Perhaps it is the gentle color medley or the quiet flow of the planting that makes this garden so memorable. But, more likely, the garden's success leans strongly on the unique idea of

training wisteria vines into their whimsical three-tiered tree form. That concept was the brainchild of William H. Frederick, Jr., a landscape architect who served as President of Longwood's Board of Trustees. Thomas Church designed the stage, but Mr. Frederick filled it with actors.

In this youth, Mr. Frederick saw tree wisterias grown at Stillpond, the estate of Mrs. William K. du Pont. Those august vines painted the sort of vision that one can never forget. And, through the years, Frederick often remembered the graceful majesty of their loosely swaying blossoms. Wishing to recapture the effect, he patiently experimented with pruning techniques until he had devised a foolproof method of training a three-tiered wisteria tree. His techniques are practiced every summer as gardeners prune the Longwood wisterias gently into shape.

The three-tiered wisterias are actually vines, coaxed over time to assume a treelike stance. When the vines were planted, each was supported by a strong metal stake imbedded below the soil in a foothold of cement. Then, the gardeners waited patiently while the vines made

Lush lavender cascades brush a powder blue bed of forget-me-nots.

headway. For five years following the initial planting, only minimal pruning was accomplished while each vine was allowed to form its sturdy trunk. When the main stem had grown thirty-six inches from the ground, five or six side shoots were allowed to sprout while the central trunk continued its journey upward. Thirty-six inches from the first crown another set of side shoots was allowed to make growth. Finally, following another two feet of growth, the final upper layer was coaxed to form the crown. Even in maturity the pruning work continues; the side shoots are pruned back yearly to stimulate blossoms and discipline the tree into shape. At Longwood, gardeners mount ladders to accomplish the clipping after the last blossom has fallen in late June or early July.

Those gigantic sculptures stand a stately ten feet or taller in height. Every May, they send their lengthy chains of lazy blossoms showering down in curtains of color. Without the competition of entangled side shoots to obstruct their downward journey, the flowering streamers fall freely and the slightest breeze sets them dancing. In that open canopy, sun rays can nourish each branch and guarantee blossoms on a vine that is not always willing to bloom freely. At the same time, the stern pruning forces the tree to send all its strength into those few branches. The tree wisterias produce cascades of pea-shaped blooms that are larger, longer, and plumper than any other wisterias at Longwood.

Although there is much to see at Longwood as spring melts into summer, most visitors remember May as wisteria time. Perhaps it is the whisper of wisteria's soft colors framed in a meadow of forget-me-nots; perhaps it is the combined perfume of their aromatic flowers. In May, Longwood is wrapped in wisteria.

Trained against a pergola, wisteria sends its strong trunk wandering upward.

A Rhapsody of White

A white garden never sleeps; it shines brilliantly at midnight and it sparkles at high noon. But twilight is its brightest hour. Gardens filled with ghostly spires of pure white foxtail lilies *(Eremurus himalaicus)*, lacy *Astilbe* 'Irrlicht', milky-white phlox, or cottony clouds of feverfew are more dazzling after dark than in broad daylight.

Born in the nineteenth century when fair gardeners dared not risk darkening their lily-white complexions by stepping outside in midday, moon gardens were designed to wax vibrant at midnight and in the delicate mists of dawn. Pristine white flowers became more popular than their gaily clad kin. White camellias, creamy gardenias, and tender white climbing roses were favored above all.

Anyone who ventures out to wade in beds of white blossoms after dusk discovers still another secret captive in those platinum petals. From their pristine lips, a fragrance whispers, calling creatures of the night. Moths and other fluttery evening insects come to drink their sweet nectar. Other ivory blooms perfume the air by day, coaxing bees and butterflies to sample their wares. White is the color that cloaks most of the world's most legendary perfume flowers. Jasmines, tuberoses, stephanotis, lilies, and citrus all send their intoxicating aromas floating from deep silver throats.

White flowers never lack color; like pearls on a strand, the petals pick up the blues of evening and reflect the yellow rays of dawn. A gentle streak of pink piercing a white gladiolus's heart waxes particularly poetic when no other colors compete; a gentle tinge of pink frosting touching the tips of dahlias blushes all the more modestly against a field of white. Like snowflakes in midsummer, a white garden dapples both dawn and dusk with a gentle blanket of blossoms.

Dawn's early light illuminates a bouyant bed of dahlias, phlox, cosmos, and Nicotiana sylvestris.

A spray of gladiolus is etched with pink.

Pompons of white dahlias are frosted with pink.

The yellow rays of dawn are reflected in this hydrangea spire.

A creamy-white rose unfurls its petals.

A White Garden at Cranbrook

Throughout the winter, the grounds are always scattered with camellias.

The chaste camellia's pure and spotless bloom,
That boasts no fragrance, and conceals no thorn.

William Roscoe

A COLLECTOR'S PARADISE
THE HUNTINGTON BOTANICAL GARDENS

*I*n December, when most gardens slip into seasonal slumber, the camellias at the Huntington Botanical Gardens slowly awaken. Nurtured by the soft sun of a California winter, plump buds burst into frilly petals, studding shiny green leaves with touches of delicate color. At first, the camellia garden is dappled only with shy blossoms scattered here or there. Gradually, as the weeks slip deeper into wintertime, more tight buds

swell to let loose their puff of petals. Finally, the North Vista of the Huntington Botanical Garden is swathed in a harmony of flora's most subtle shades.

Above the camellias, tall fan palms offer their tufts to the sky and native oaks cast a soft net of shade. Below the camellias, mounds of neatly clipped azaleas crouch, ready to slip into blossom when winter melts into California spring. Among those shiny-leaved trees, a procession of

A camellia bud sparkles with the dewdrops of a misty morning.

seventeenth-century statues flanks either side of an emerald lawn. Bacchus, Aphrodite, Perseus clutching a writhing Medusa, and dozens of other mythological figures step out like stony white specters amidst an airy mass of camellias. For one enchanted moment, fantasy borders on the divine.

Huntington is a collection of many breathtaking moments. Set in San Marino, where the climate permits all sorts of sorcery, Huntington is a garden of varied faces. Once the home of Henry E. Huntington, an official of the Southern Pacific railroad, the 207-acre estate combines an obsession for diversity with a flair for design.

Henry Huntington was an incurable collector. He acquired entire libraries of rare volumes and aggressively sought British art from the Georgian period. When Henry brought his new bride, Arabella,

to San Marino in 1913, the collector's urge branched into the botanical realm. At first, Henry dabbled in commercial pomology, planting orchards of avocados, oranges, and apricots. But as he labored to breed more fruitful cultivars, he discovered a deep fascination for flora. The gardens sweeping around the Beaux Arts mansion reflect the Huntington hunger for beauty. Every coveted botanical acquisition also speaks of Henry's instincts as a collector. Henry personally oversaw the assembly of a bristling cactus and succulent collection. But the softer niches on the grounds—the Rose Garden and the camellia paths—were planted for Arabella.

The craftsmanship of nature whispers throughout Huntington. Everywhere, plants are displayed amidst works of art. Statues, fountains, and temples are tucked here and there. They accent the contours of the land and lure visitors from one grand landscape to the next. They capture the first glow of sunrise and glisten by dusk's last rays. Pergolas and archways link gardens, softening the diversity of plant life, extending the lushness in a series of encores until it fades into the next scene.

Botanical wonders are given equal footing with creations carved of marble and travertine. Silhouetted against neatly trimmed greensward, flowering trees such as the silk floss tree (*Chorisia insignis*), magnolias, and statuesque palms step forward as individuals, while groupings of more diminutive blossoming shrubs are massed closely to project a unified voice. Colors are mingled and softly graduated, while forms are balanced by complementary bedfellows. Design turns the collection from a static and pompous museum of astonishingly rare specimens into living, performing art. All the while, careful composition permits each rare species and every deftly bred cultivar to shine as a masterpiece.

Huntington may sparkle in the rays of the midsummer sun, but the gardens are most alluring when they lie half shrouded in the mists of a winter rain shower. Then they play a coquettish game of enticement and reward, hiding delightful secrets in the fog ahead, only to unfold their splendor gradually when explored. The statues of the North Vista wade knee-deep in vaporous clouds, their rising torsos illuminated by a feeble shaft of light. The camellias seem suspended in air. An immense Italian fountain, featuring cavorting dolphins and spouting sea creatures, is only a vague outline on the horizon; the distant San Gabriel Mountains have disappeared entirely.

The Shakespearean Garden is only steps away from the North Vista. A panoply of bloomers mentioned by the bard in bold shades floods crescent-shaped beds. Mullein, sea holly, daylilies, daisies, salvias, and butterburs cavort in the central bed. A riot of impertinent pansies, bright ranunculus, and relatively subdued irises stands on the sidelines. The fiery colors of transient poppies demand attention for a few weeks in early summer, before shattering into a mass of crinkled petals.

Wherever one wanders, statues set the mood. Beyond the Shakespearean beds, stone and marble artifacts slow the pace from frenzied to contemplative. Broad but feathery Montezuma cypresses (*Taxodium mucronatum*) sway gracefully, weeping over an eighteenth-century French stone Temple of Love, softening the transition from the ebullient primary shades of Elizabethan annuals into the hushed pastels of the rose beds. Suddenly, the theme is romantic, whispered from the satiny lips of every rosebud.

Arbors embrace walkways, wrapping visitors in lush garlands of dawn pink 'Belle of Portugal', blushing peach 'Shot Silk', and creamy 'Snow Bird'. The aroma heightens with every step as the world is steeped in attar of roses. Profusion reigns. In autumn, scattered blossoms punctuate waves of neatly pruned, three-foot bushes. And from that moment on, the display builds volume until, by mid-April, the Rose Garden peaks in a flood of flowers reflected overhead by blooming magnolias.

Framed in a lush lawn, monochromatic beds filled with sunset-hued and ivory floribundas set the geometric stage. Not far away, beside a latticework pergola, the legacy of roses is laid out in a chronological progression. Behind squared hedges of Greek myrtle (*Myrtus communis* 'Compacta'), deftly blended beds of 'Old Blush' (circa 1793), 'Slater's Crimson China' (circa 1790), and the intensely perfumed damask 'Leda' (introduced prior to 1827)

One of the Pleasures at the Huntington

On the North Vista, seventeenth-century statues with mythological themes step from amidst the camellias. They originally came from an estate in Padua, Italy, where the soft limestone deteriorated, erasing all evidence of their identities. Of the two dozen statues, only Bacchus, Aphrodite, and Perseus are easily recognizable. Close to the entry of the North Vista, a temple holds a playful nineteenth-century marble statue entitled "Cupid Blindfolding Youth," opposite, lower left.

blossom in one magnificent rush of color. Modern hybrids extend the performance. Steeped in perfume and clothed in silky petals, the pageant evolves, climaxing with the legendary tea roses represented by such luminaries as 'Catherine Mermet' (circa 1869) and 'Lady Hillingdon' (circa 1910).

Roses accent the architectural elements in the garden. 'Mermaid' climbs to the top of an open dome, shading a marble bench. Surrounding the Temple of Love, 'French Lace', an exquisitely fragrant floribunda, sets off the stone work with its ivory petals, and a border of the scented parma violet 'Princess of Wales' muffles the roses in a deep purple foil.

Refinements are continually honed and new hybrids are welcomed into experimental beds. Presently, rosarians are evaluating a collection of David Austin's English roses—a series of modern hybrids that embody all the aromatic endowments of heirloom varieties but imitate none of their finicky traits. 'Wise Portia', 'Fair Bianca', and 'Tamora' lie in neat mounds, bristling with a continual array of recurrent blossoms. However, the test beds have revealed some disappointments—'Constance Spry' and 'Yellow Charles Austin' proved too rambunctious, stretching inelegantly skyward under the intense California sun.

Alongside a rose-interlaced pergola, the Herb Garden spreads its mounds of greens and silvers. Traversed by brick herringbone paths, each geometric bed is packed with a profusion of aromatic herbs. Accenting the center, silver-leaved thymes creep around an eighteenth-century wrought-iron wellhead and borders of rosemary, lacy wormwood, lavender, and rugosa and sweetbriar roses buffer the garden on all sides.

Within the garden, each herb bed explores a

Camellias are famed for their profusion.

Sun rays gently touch the pale pink petals of a peony-form camellia.

personal theme. In a bed sprawling with herbs used for liqueurs and winery, hop vines (*Humulus lupulus*) climb energetically up bamboo poles above *Geum urbanum* (once used to keep ale from souring), *Myrtus communis* 'Boetica' (the blue berries impart their flavor to wines), *Artemisia absinthium* (notorious as the main constituent in absinthe), and red carnations (a single blossom will lace liqueurs with a hint of clove). Perfume herbs nestle into several beds. The mingled aromas of *Iris pallida*, *Gardenia jasminoides* 'Prostrata', plumeria, evening primrose, clary sage, saffron, jonquil, mignonette, patchouli, vetiver, and heliotrope form a heady brew drawn forth by the brilliant southwestern sun.

The rose pergola finishes its journey at a tall stucco fence guarded by a formidable pair of stone lions. Visitors who dare slip past its gates discover the hidden Japanese Garden sprawling in the valley below. Dominated by a vermilion moon bridge spanning a pond where tame *koi* dart between lily pads and sweet flag, the garden is studded with a ceremonial bell, pagodas, and votive stones, set amongst evergreens in verdant shades. Spring finds the lush valley framed by wisteria draping from the porch of an authentic Japanese house. In April, the contours of the flowing landscape are accented with blossoming peaches, azaleas, and the snowy white fringe tree (*Chionanthus retusus*). During other seasons, the landscape is a study in mossy greens unfettered by the distraction of flowers. Every vista is meant to

reveal an intimacy with nature. And every carefully composed setting is designed to promote inward contemplation.

From the Japanese Garden, the path forks to roam through a forest of Australian shrubs or walk beside slopes carpeted with *Trachelospermum asiaticum*, gazania, Acapulco daisy (*Zinnia maritma*), salvias, and other subtropical bloomers. Farther away, a waterfall plummets beyond the boulders and bromeliads of a profuse jungle habitat. Then, just as abruptly, the waterfall's fury is silenced in the still waters of a series of lily ponds below.

The path meanders back to its point of departure through a forest of cacti and succulents. Basking among red lava rocks, golden barrel cacti glow and silver mammillarias shimmer. Crassulas sprawl onto the walkway while stately yuccas bristle in the background. The desert garden, with its collection of twenty-five thousand barbed beauties, portrays the thorns of horticultural romance.

Every eclectic garden at Huntington murmurs of a flowery infatuation. The legions of absurd cacti, the avenues of divine camellias, and the pergolas of dainty roses are all steeped in ardor. At Huntington, many themes merge subtly. The diverse gardens are unified in their exultation of nature.

By the 1840s, camellias were all the vogue in Britain. Queen Victoria wrote to a relative, "If we have no mountains to boast of, we have the sea, which is ever enjoyable, and we have camellias."

Camellias at the Huntington

Exquisite as a Camellia

On bright summer days, the North Vista of the Huntington Botanic Garden stares outward, sending its gaze to a gurgling fountain at the garden's end and farther to the San Gabriel Mountains etched on the horizon. But during the depths of winter, the North Vista looks inward, focusing on the camellias that line its perimeter. They stand graceful and grand on both sides of a broad lawn, towering proudly above mounds of dwarf azaleas.

In summer, the North Vista's camellias slip into the background, simply providing an evergreen screen behind rows of glistening white statues. But when autumn settles in, they suddenly become bold. Their buds expand, slowly growing rounder and rounder still. Then, just when it seems they can swell no more, the buds dramatically pop into pompoms of petals. 'Pink Perfection', 'Donckelarii', 'Glen 40', and 'Arajishi' are all studded with color. For the rest of the season, the garden is awash with a concert of a hundred floral notes.

Winter is the camellia's shining moment. Other plants shiver and pout while California's fickle temperatures fluctuate. But regardless of the weather, the camellias loyally erupt into blossom, providing a spellbinding sight. Each flower might measure three to four inches from edge to edge. And those immense blossoms do not lose detail as they gain girth. Each is a masterpiece of color, a soft sculpture crafted of gently curving petals swirling toward a satiny center. The sheer abundance multiplies the impact a hundredfold. When the camellias are in full flower, the garden is transformed into a spontaneous pageant, strewn with

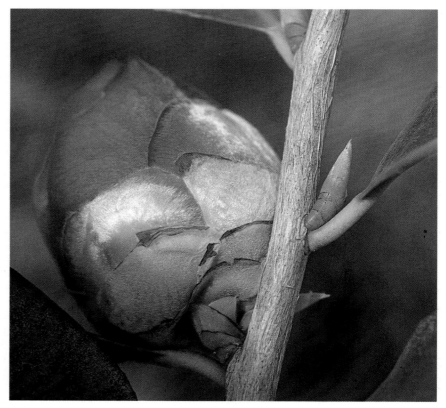

Nearly ready to burst, a camellia bud shows its first hints of color.

Amidst single and frilly semidouble red camellias lies a luscious, rare pink and white Higo camellia. Higo hybrids were cultivated for centuries as traditional flowers of the Japanese samurai.

blossoms like a blitz of confetti tossed to the trees.

Camellias are the roses of winter. They are serious and sensual flowers. Like roses, they do not play lightly with one's affections. But, unlike rosebuds, camellias prolong their performance with style throughout the season. The shiny-leaved trees faithfully unfold bud after bud, adding to the breadth of pompoms as the season steals by. From October until May, there is a continual promenade of early, midseason, and finally late bloomers producing their frilly flowers before bowing out. All the while, spent flowers poetically tumble to the ground while seemingly still in the flush of youth. The trees are bedecked, the ground is carpeted, and the ghostly white statues wade among the profusion. Throughout the winter, the North Vista of Huntington maintains a surrealistic ecstasy.

The North Vista is the Huntington's most theatric camellia garden. On its open stage, a few chosen prima donnas swirl and pirouette to an appreciative audience. But the main cast of characters—the camellia chorus —actually waits backstage. Not far from the North Vista, other camellia-lined walkways

beckon. The bulk of the collection is planted on ten rolling acres, where large numbers of shrubs can frolic unhampered. Huntington boasts seventeen hundred different camellia cultivars growing on its lands, and most can be seen in a forest overlooking a steep canyon.

Azaleas crouch at the entryway of the camellia walk. A set of cherubic statues politely ushers visitors in, coaxing all who pass to pause and explore the winding alleyway. The path travels deeper into that enchanted forest, strolling beside a hillside of small-leaved, spreading *Camellia sasanqua* cultivars and wandering leisurely through groves of straight and tall *Camellia japonica* hybrids in every imaginable blushing shade. Planted in a nook known as the species lane, thirty camellia species including the rare sulphur yellow *Camellia chrysantha*, the bona fide tea *Camellia sinensis*, and the intoxicatingly fragrant *Camellia lutchuensis* bask in dappled shade. The predominance of velvety pinks is delightful as flowers escort the walkway on all sides. For several months in midwinter, the world is wrapped in a mass of pompons suspended on shiny-leaved trees and the rambling

walkway is strewn with plush blossoms falling nearly unblemished underfoot.

The Huntington camellia collection began with 'Pink Perfection', a profuse, rose-shaped *Camellia japonica* cultivar found growing beside the San Marino mansion when Henry Huntington purchased the estate in 1903. The first camellias to arrive in Europe from the Orient were also *Camellia japonica* cultivars. Unfortunately, the introduction proved to be an awkward moment in both botanical and diplomatic history. In the 1730s, the British were anxiously expecting a shipment of tea trees (*Camellia sinensis*) when Chinese merchants substituted the closely related *Camellia japonica* instead. That delightful, frilly-flowered tree took Britain completely by surprise, but after the initial shock, the British welcomed and eventually worshipped the divine shrub. It was a romance that waxed and waned in fervor throughout the centuries.

The prototypical European camellia was entrusted to Lord Petre of Essex to be grown in his greenhouse. There, the small tree was pampered and coddled until it finally perished from the heat that was increased for its

Dappled sun slips into Huntington's North Vista to illuminate the simple splendor of a semidouble white camellia.

Camellia 'Alba Plena' was the first double rose form camellia seen in the West.

Camellias are famed for their subtle shades such as this luscious blend of pink and apricot hues.

benefit. Lord Petre died shortly thereafter of smallpox, although it was widely rumored that the nobleman was mortally wounded by his failure. If the camellia's auspicious introduction had not garnered it sufficient renown, Lord Petre's tragedy successfully turned all eyes toward the dramatic flowering shrub. In addition to gathering public interest, the episode also taught future growers an invaluable lesson: camellias can endure all kinds of conditions, but they will not tolerate warmth in winter. Early indoor gardeners rapidly discovered that camellias disdain warm living rooms. Their promising buds drop unopened, or they stubbornly refuse to set buds at all when temperatures exceed 55°F at night. In the height of their infatuation for the flower, the Victorians provided those luscious trees with greenhouses specifically designed to accommodate their broad dimensions and carefully engineered to furnish chilly—but not frigid—nights.

Not long afterward, gardeners in temperate regions of this country began to plant camellias outdoors, and they witnessed the most ravishing rewards. Nothing can compare to the impact of camellias planted where they can

gently spread their tall, blossom-laden stems toward the sky. Stately and tall, japonica camellias send their branches stretching upward with a strong vertical thrust. The dense foliage is always thick, waxy, and glistening, as if freshly shined. Few insects pester them; no diseases mar their beauty. Camellias are invariably impeccably clad. They can be the epitome of elegance and formality. They can stand straight and sophisticated in unwavering lines like a cotillion of debutantes all in ruffled wardrobe, or in less stringently structured plantings, they can link branches in a graceful waltz.

Camellias are masters of disguise. They masquerade as many different flowers. The petals of single blossoms dance around a nest of yellow stamens dusted with pollen. Formal double types open their buds in a ballet reminiscent of an unravelling rosebud. The peony form has a fluff of incurved petals at its center, and the anemone form holds its broad outer petals away from a fringed inner tuft. Every shade of white, whisper pink, deep rose, and blushing red is represented in those thin petals, while streaks, flecks, and picotee edges add still another dimension.

In the glistening North Vista, sun-tolerant japonicas such as 'Pink Perfection', 'Arajishi', 'Blood of China', 'Lady Clare', 'Covina', and 'Daikagura' line the avenue. But most *Camellia japonica* cultivars prefer shelter from the sun's strongest rays. Above Huntington's camellia canyon, native oaks (*Quercus agrifolia*) and assorted maples spread their dappled canopy over the japonicas in summer, shielding them from the sun, while their bare branches allow winter's softer light to penetrate unhindered. On the forest floor, the ground cover sprawls. *Lamiastrum* 'Herman's Pride', violets, yarrow, and *Mazus reptans* all roam around the ankles of camellias, half hiding their wide trunks.

Underfoot, a slightly acid soil forms a bed for the roots. A pH of 6.0 is optimal for camellias. When the trees were originally planted, each was provided with a padding of peat moss in the hole it would call home, but the peat has long since broken down to merge with the sandy California soil. Now, the forest depends on fallen oak leaves to acidify the soil. As companions, other acid-loving shrubs are sprinkled in along the hillside. Rhododendrons, azaleas, and mountain laurels play merrily amongst the camellias.

Sprinklers send rushing water jets rotating frantically on the canyon floor during California's inevitable midsummer droughts, but the camellias could survive without daily waterings. They are not difficult to please. Camellias are famed for their fortitude. In the Orient, venerable old camellias, bent and weighty with age, cling to rocks close to the ocean's edge, enduring winds and lean soil but blossoming stoically nonetheless. Camellias cheerfully tolerate downpour and droughts, but good drainage is imperative.

Other camellias share the canyon with the japonicas. Standing on a hillside of their own, *Camellia sasanqua* cultivars expand their gracefully spreading branches to interlace twigs. The sasanquas are the harbingers of winter's prolonged performance. Long before the first japonica opens, sasanquas wrap their small-leaved branches from elbow to wrist with wispy puffs of apple blossom-like flowers.

Sasanquas are not as dramatic as japonicas—their blossoms are not as ornate or immense— but they have their own special

Dew kisses a promising bud.

shining graces. Swaying their arms slowly in the breezes, sasanquas impart a deliciously subtle aroma into the late autumn air, suffusing the garden with both delicate hues and delicious perfume—and fragrance is a rare virtue in camellias. They are the hush before the blizzard; they are the prelude to the symphony.

Sasanquas prefer more light than their relatives, so sun shafts are permitted to fall unfettered on the sasanqua hillside. The rays gently caress the small blooms and illuminate their colors into a massive conflagration announc-

ing the arrival of winter. The japonicas will soon join in.

When the roses are resting and the wisteria is expecting signs of spring, the camellias at the Huntington slowly unfold their drama. There is something irrepressibly voluptuous about the performance. Prim and proper, always impeccably attired, camellias are the essence of all that is lovely about gardening. Burdened with their frills and flowers for half the year, camellias breathe warmth into winter and then run headlong into spring.

The Tradition of Camellia Portraits

Flowers have always inspired artists to immortalize a moment of nature. They take up their brushes, they brandish pencils, and they stir paint. They contemplate form, texture, and the subtleties of color. Then, they set to work—toiling to distill the essence of a blossom and the soul of a bud in a few deft strokes.

They choose all forms of media and focus on every sort of subject. A tuft of grass or a shattered petal is sufficient to inspire some artists. Other artists seek the most complex blossoms in creation to pique their pens and paintbrushes. No matter what their method or model might be,

botanical artists all tackle similar problems. Their mission is to capture and hold one moment in a flower's brief lifetime. The transience of nature is their challenge, and they all race to render a likeness before petals drop. But skillful masterpieces show much more. Not only does a truly inspired drawing portray the present, it also provides some hint of the past and future of the flower. After all, time is the essence of botany: yesterday a bud was swelling; and tomorrow its colors will fade.

Some blossoms beg to be immortalized. A rose is irresistible to artists. Peonies, with their many poetic petals, are equally tempting. Chrysanthemums, orchids, and calla lilies invariably attract artists. And once an artist has discovered an especially intriguing subject, he or she returns time and time again to look once more, to explore all aspects of that theme. Different balances of light, changing seasons, and different cultivars all must be analyzed. Claude Monet was fascinated by the many facets of water

lilies, Childe Hassam studied the brilliance of poppies, and Pierre-Joseph Redouté recorded the ethereal essence of roses. When camellias arrived in Europe, they took their place among the world's most enigmatic and carefully studied flowers. Camellias inspired countless artists to take up brushes in an attempt to capture their subtle charms.

In the Orient, camellias had been associated with arts and crafts for centuries. In Japan, their image appeared on silk screens; it was woven into robes, painted on porcelain, and embellished on fans. Screens, scrolls, enamels, and wood carvings all attempted to capture the camellia's elusive beauty. In China, camellias were rendered in embroidery, lacquer, cloisonné, silk screens, and scrolls.

When camellias appeared in the West, many craftsmen paid homage to the delicate, fleeting beauty of those heavenly flowers. In contrast to the stylized renderings of Oriental artisans, European artists took a painstakingly realistic approach. They studied

Few monographs caught their sheen like Camellias *edited by Beryl Leslie Urquhart and illustrated by Paul Jones (*Camellia reticulata *'Tzepao', above left) and Raymond Booth (*Camellia japonica *'Robert Fortune,' above right and a Higo camellia opposite).*

the flowers; they contemplated the lay of each petal and the etching of veins on every leaf. In their art, flowers were depicted in minute detail. Every fleck and variation in color was exposed; every subtle shadow was revealed. European artists scrutinized camellias with the rapt attention that often accompanies novelty. Europe's love affair with camellias was both intense and sharply focused.

Artist after artist labored to capture the unique glow of light on a camellia's glossy foliage or the sheen of a ray as it brushed the flower's soft petals. They balanced one blossom form against the other in a medley of different floral colors. They focused closely on a single flower and then stood back to paint an entire bouquet.

For many decades, most gardeners knew camellias only as they were portrayed in paintings, and they hungered for another glimpse of those splendid flowers. Volume after volume was published to glorify the flower, and each was greeted by an insatiable public. In 1819, Clara Maria Pope was among the first Europeans to illustrate a monograph on camellias, and her

prints set the trend of focusing on a head-and-shoulders portrait of the blossom. The precedent was followed by the nurseryman Ambroise Verschaffelt, who published a thirteen-volume set entitled *Nouvelle Iconographie des Camélias*, illustrated with no fewer than 623 color plates. Redouté also turned his talents toward camellias, publishing *Les Camélias* and executing a series of paintings to catalogue the twelve thousand plants in the private collection of an Italian camellia enthusiast. Magazines also attempted to satisfy their readers' craving for camellias with full-color, hand-painted illustrations utilizing the talents of lesser-known artists. Before the average gardener ever met a growing, blossoming camellia face to face, the flower was already comfortably familiar.

Like the rose, the camellia never lost its attraction for artists. Time has strengthened the bond. Hybridizers continually create variations in color and form, while artists work right alongside, sketching and painting the ever-broadening mass of models. They draw and they learn secrets. Flowers reveal intimacies to artists, and they render them in paint and ink.

Celia Thaxter's beds, above, sported orange poppies and nasturtiums next to pink dianthus.
Single dahlia types, opposite, she called "king's flowers . . . stately and splendid."

At bird peep, as the country folk have a charming way of calling the break of day, I am in my dear garden,—planting and transplanting. . . .

Celia Thaxter

A WRITER'S PASSION
CELIA THAXTER'S ISLAND GARDEN

When the sea is calm surrounding the Isles of Shoals, the aquamarine waters bristle with small boats bobbing lazily up and down. The foam-capped waves lovingly caress the rocky shores of Appledore, the largest of the Isles of Shoals off the coast of Maine and New Hampshire, where the blossoms in Celia Thaxter's island garden sparkle and sway.

Even in fine weather, Appledore is a solitary setting. The ninety-five-acre island is scattered with little else but goldenrod, wild mustard, and other rambunctious wildflowers running in drifts amongst the gleaming granite rocks. Nothing stands taller than the choke cherry—no forests of stately trees grace Appledore. Instead, the elderberry and sumac huddle together in dense thickets while brambles clutch at the bankings. Appledore is a wind-beaten and sun-nourished land accented by ruby-throated rambling roses and punctuated by the sea gull's haunting cry.

But there, carved from the granite and brambles, the island garden proudly spreads its riotous carpet of color. Silhouetted starkly against the sea and sky, the small (15 × 50 foot) plot braves the elements to

Celia Thaxter's Island View

burst into blossom season after season. Sprouting from a series of prim, rectangular beds, blossoms barrage the senses, pouring their fragrance into the sea air, scattering the adjacent rocks with petals. Planted in drills to sing in unison, Shirley poppies and sweet peas jubilantly spread their branches and splash the island with color. Underlying the roar of those sizzling shades, a quiet rhythm rules the garden. When one bloom shatters, another takes up the tempo. And when the breezes play, the flower-heads do tempestuous dances, bowing and bending, forming a crazy patchwork with their neighbors. Without a doubt, this is a poet's garden.

Years ago, the glint of those blossoms against the glow of the ocean inspired countless verses. Long before she ever touched pen to paper, Celia Laighton

Celia wrote, "Just beyond the Sweet Peas I could see my strong white Lilies springing up . . . with the splendid hardy Larkspurs behind them, promising a wealth of white and gold and azure by and by."

began composing poetic plantings. Her father, a well-respected businessman in Portsmouth, New Hampshire, succumbed to the lure of the ocean and took a job as a lighthouse keeper on White Island when Celia was merely four years old. She later remembered those early formative years, "A lonely child, living on the lighthouse island ten miles from the mainland, every blade of grass was precious in my sight, and I began a little garden when not more than five years old."

In 1848, when Celia was twelve years old, the family moved to Appledore to build a large seasonal hotel. There, she was schooled in the secrets of both soil and sea. She discovered that hungry migrating birds—the bobolinks, kingbirds, orioles, and purple finches—could strip her garden bare in a few brief hours. She received a practical education: she was tutored by Levi Thaxter, a handsome Harvard graduate. At the age of sixteen, she married her tutor and moved to the mainland.

Too homesick to remain landlocked for long, Celia returned to Appledore every summer to tend her island garden. When April was still young, she packed her belongings—books, houseplants, and trays of seedlings planted in fragile eggshells rather than pots—aboard a steam tug to brave the choppy water between Portsmouth and Appledore. There she found a cottage waiting, with her flower beds stretching in the front yard already prepared.

Spring comes late to the Isles of Shoals. But by the end of May, the soil is warmed by the island sun and ready to receive tender seedlings. Nothing was sown directly in the soil; every blossom was transplanted from seeds started on the mainland in February. The design was simplicity itself. Celia wrote, "I have not the room to experiment with rockworks and ribbon-borders and the like, nor should I do it even if I had all the room in the world."

While daylight shone, Celia could be found weeding, staking, transplanting, and primping her flower beds. Every morning she awoke at 4:30 A.M. and was busy about her "bird-blest and persecuted little garden" long before dawn broke. Often she stole into the garden by moonlight to lay little barricades of lime against her arch enemies, the slugs, which riddled her moist island beds.

Tucked inside a protective fence, she laid out nine slim rectangular beds edged with wood. Each bed was devoted to a sole stretch of one or two annuals. Shirley poppies, "like a rosy dawn, Aurora herself" tossed their petaled heads in one bed, while other rectangles were vibrant with bachelor's buttons, cleome, and California poppies.

Droves of distinguished guests strolled through the picket fence on their way to Celia's front parlor. Nathaniel Hawthorne, William Dean Howells, William Morris Hunt, John Greenleaf Whittier, Henry Ward Beecher, Samuel Longfellow, and Childe Hassam all paid visits to the island garden. Through the cottage's curtains of white wisteria and Japanese hops *(Humulus japonicus)* floated the notes of Celia's grand piano mingling with the laughter of a parlor filled with garrulous company.

In 1894, Celia Thaxter turned her pen from poetry and wrote *An Island Garden*, a book that immortalized the beds that spread before her front door. Childe Hassam, who spent many summers patiently capturing Celia's poppies with his Impressionistic brushstrokes, illustrated the text with a series of whimsical watercolors. Tragically, the book was completed only months before Celia passed away at the age of fifty-nine. For many years afterward, members of her family faithfully maintained the island garden until, in 1914, a raging fire consumed the hotel, Celia's cottage, and most of the other buildings on Appledore. The island was left to the

*Zinnias, sweet rocket (*Hesperis matronalis*), marigolds, nicotiana, and helianthus jubilantly intertwine, above. Celia described the eschscholzia poppy, opposite above, as "a diamond of flame in a cup of gold," and wrote of ". . . the bed of Pansies," opposite below, "set out yesterday was bright with promise, every little planting holding itself gladly erect."*

granite rocks, to the wildflowers, and to the sea gulls circling overhead.

But lured by the temptation to recreate the garden that once beckoned an era of eminent Victorians, the Shoals Marine Laboratory and local garden clubs combined forces in 1977 to restore the garden exactly as it was when Celia Thaxter tended the island beds. Salvaged from the sumac and witch grass that claimed the soil in the interim, the garden now stands proud and brilliant against the sparkling sea. The fence again shepherds its flock of luxuriant blossoms, but now chicken wire is stapled to the fence boards and buried a foot underground to secure the garden from its newest foe—a hoard of hungry muskrats that have recently taken up residence on Appledore. Seedlings are raised yearly on the mainland and ferried in pots just as Celia once transported her garden in eggshells to its island home.

As soon as the plants are slipped into the soil, they spring up and unfold spritely colors just as they did under Celia's gentle care. The sun-washed beds again spill with coreopsis, fragrant mignonette, asters, Shirley poppies, and eschscholzia poppies. The fence is once more festooned with plump sweet peas, a tangle of honeysuckle, and wayward wild cucumbers *(Echinocystis lobata)*.

There is something very brave about this island garden that defies the storms of the sea and the winds of change. There is something enchanting about its precocious colors standing starkly outlined by the aquamarine sea. In its solitary world serenaded solely by sea gulls and lapping waves, Celia Thaxter's garden is always proudly sparkling.

This Everlasting Garden

Brilliantly colored snapdragons wait to be plucked and dried.

Potpourri is the essence of a dozen summers carefully preserved. It is the synthesis of the season's many fleeting scents and subtle pigments all tumbled together and held captive in time. Stir potpourri gently and a multitude of precious moments are recalled. The pungence of a newly mown hayfield, the vibrance of a bouquet chock-full of freshly opened carnations, the gentle musk of a milkweed meadow buzzing with the labors of so many bees—all of summer's delights are distilled in a bowl.

Gardeners have been capturing the scents of summer since antiquity. Originally, dried herbs were strewn on chamber floors to perfume the air. They were tucked in linens to lend freshness to the fabric and hung among clothes to repel moths. But, somehow, the craft fell into disuse when the twentieth century arrived. The brash smell of synthetic aerosols suddenly permeated the places where pure potpourri once spread its gentle scents.

Potpourri had slipped into the realms of a lost art when Sharon Ackland, a young horticultural student, discovered the craft while traveling through the perfume districts of France. It was the history of potpourri that immediately intrigued her, but she also suspected that potpourri might present a sterling opportunity to express her many horticultural and artistic talents.

Upon her return to this country, Sharon began experimenting with mixtures, always attempting to capture a certain elusive summer mood. At first, she followed Colonial recipes, but with gained confidence, she began blending her own artistic compositions of balanced textures, colors, and aromas. Before long, La Petite Fleur, Sharon's potpourri busi-

The dried flower collage is an artistic creation. Sumptuous colors play together, but the secret lies in the greenery that falls like lacework between the blossoms.

Captured in acetate boxes, each potpourri is covered with a masterpiece of carefully arranged dried flowers, whispering of summer's pigments.

Bedded out with a mulch of salt hay, an exuberant chorus of summer's finest flowers wait to be harvested.

ness, was born. Since 1977, La Petite Fleur has been capturing the essence of summer in a series of delectable potpourris.

The potpourris blended by La Petite Fleur strive to capture the harmony of nature. Field and forest scents form the basis of their brews. Such wildlings as meadowsweet, sweet clover, yarrow, tansy, and sweet woodruff provide the prevailing note. To those earthy scents, the effusion of the herb garden is blended by adding caraway, thyme, orange mint, costmary, lemon verbena, scented geraniums, and dozens of other aromatic plants. A hint of the exotic is introduced with tonka beans, quassia chips, cloves, and vanilla beans. Finally, undiluted essential oils

are sprinkled over the top. When stirred, the result echoes all the delights of summer although the season might be months away.

There is an herb garden in southern Michigan where lavender, rosemary, gillyflower, feverfew, sweet cicely, artemisia, and curry plants (*Helichrysum angustifolium*) all flourish in the strong sun until they are plucked for La Petite Fleur's potpourri. Seventy antique roses—primarily the intensely redolent damask, gallic, and rugosa roses—produce buds that will be removed just before their moment of splendor. The herbs and roses are harvested at dawn or twilight when their oils are most vibrant. Pruning shears work rapidly as large baskets are heaped hastily

with herbs to be carried into a barn where drying screens await. There they are strewn loosely—never crowded—on the screens to dry, sheltered from the sun's scorching rays but fanned by the light breezes that creep gently through the barnboards.

Long-stemmed herbs such as lavender are tied into bunches and hung upside down from the rafters to swing slowly overhead. Depending upon the weather, a week—sometimes two—might elapse while the herbs dry. Then, each species is stored separately in airtight boxes, sealing their fragrance.

The actual blending of aromatics is ruled more by whimsy than recipe. A dozen eclectic ingredients might mingle lightly together in the final product. Rose petals, lavender blossoms, milkweed flowers, viburnum, orange mint, allspice berries, sweet myrtle, and cardamon seed all combine in La Petite Fleur's gillyflower blend. The herbs are then stirred with tonka beans, sandalwood chips, cloves, and nutmeg before being anointed with the essence of rose, carnation, and lavender. The final brew serenades the senses with a spicy, rosy elixir accented by a whisper of the tropics. To enliven the tawny colors of potpourri, an artful collage of painstakingly preserved dried flowers crowns each container, enticing everyone to explore inside. Each blossom

is captured at its moment of perfection; each looks as if it had just been plucked from the vine. Roses hold their youthful blush, daffodils trumpet brazenly as if still poised on the stem, and snapdragons have the same insolent sauciness that they displayed in the heat of the summer. Throughout many changing seasons, those blossoms remain locked in time.

All the dried flowers strewn on top of the potpourri boxes once grew, budded, and blossomed in La Petite Fleur's one-acre Michigan garden. There, rows of marigolds, zinnias, hollyhocks, lavender, larkspur, and delphiniums dance and sway until they are

plucked at their moment of personal ripeness. Fading and imperfect flowers are passed over, but youthful buds are often harvested before the summer sun steals their luster.

Silica gel waits for them in the kitchen, previously heated on long trays for an hour in an oven set at 250° to completely remove the gel's moisture. A layer of that gel coats the bottom of an airtight container, forming a bed for a layer of freshly plucked blossoms. And another two-inch layer of gel blankets the blooms while they are drying in their closed chamber. Thinly petaled blossoms such as daisies and columbine require only five days to dry completely. Thicker blossoms such as hyacinths, lilies, and roses might take longer. When they are ready, the blossoms look just as they did in the field, although their fragrance has vanished. They are scattered on top of the potpourri, giving the mixture vibrance.

A finished potpourri pleases all the senses. To excite its aromas, to release its captive essence one need only gently disturb the slumbering blossoms. Then, all of summer comes rushing forth to tickle a gardener's imagination and whisper the promise of a coming season.

Carefully cut, blossoms wait in baskets to be whisked into the kitchen for drying in silica gel.

In spring, daffodils rush enthusiastically down the entry drive of Longview Farm to welcome friends with a warm greeting, above.
Like lace in front of the red-sided barn, opposite, apple blossoms etch still-naked branches with a dainty frill of spring color.

But on the hill the golden-rod, and aster in the wood,
And the yellow sunflower by the brook, in autumn beauty stood.

William Cullen Bryant

A LIFETIME FRIENDSHIP WITH A GARDEN
JOANNA REED'S LONGVIEW FARM

Joanna Reed is rarely right at hand when visitors arrive at Longview Farm, so a dinner bell hangs not far from her front door with a note pinned to its lever. "Ring Me," it urges. And no one can resist the invitation. Before the full-bodied echo finishes resounding throughout the Pennsylvania hills, Joanna appears, wiping her soiled hands quickly before extending them in welcome.

From that moment on, Longview Farm feels like home. Just as Joanna's outstretched arms greet all who come, the farm also embraces everyone who turns into the flower-bordered drive. Unpretentious and yet fascinatingly diverse, witty and whimsical but never silly, Longview Farm is a country garden steeped in warm overtones. "Nothing is formal about this garden," Joanna explains as she strolls past vine-embowered corn cribs or sweeps aside roving Japanese anemones to clear a sitting spot on a cement bench. This is country at its best—deftly crafted and yet delightfully spontaneous.

Nothing is formal about the white stucco farmhouse, either. It is the sort of place where windows are always slightly ajar, letting snippets of laughter from family and house guests escape into the flower-filled terrace. It is the sort of house where doors are

Winter spreads its white blanket over the courtyard garden below Joanna's farmhouse window.

Spring is infused with rich colors and mingled with the delicious aroma of lilacs (Syringa 'Ludwig Spaeth').

invariably thrown open, coaxing all who come to make themselves comfortable in the labyrinth of cozy rooms. An occasional moth flutters in through screenless windows to punctuate lamp-lit evenings. At midday, a bumblebee might blunder past a screenless door to admire a parlor bouquet. All who enter the black-shuttered farmhouse are given a gracious reception.

Joanna's hospitality extends into the gardens as well. Thirty-seven acres lie around the house and its bleached stone, berry-trimmed barn. And every square foot holds a bounty that arrived with visitors and stayed. Longview Farm is a collector's garden. The most wondrous rarities nestle comfortably along fence rows or lean lackadaisically beside wellheads of brick to soften the no-nonsense lines of the farm. Somehow, even tropical herbs melt into the scenery when allowed to grow profusely and spread opu-

lently. Merging with the countryside, adding their distinct accent to the soft Pennsylvania drawl spoken throughout these hills, annuals and perennials of all descriptions blend together in country charm. They all become part of the farm.

There is a precious continuity about this garden. Winter, spring, summer, and fall—the land never pauses. Joanna's garden maintains its uninterrupted flow throughout all the seasons of the year. In spring, early bulbs emerge and flowering trees burst into color. In summer, daylilies punctuate footpaths while pelargoniums and begonias shimmer in the sun. Autumn is a blaze of deep reds, rich golds, and burnished browns as deciduous shrubs display their varied shades. And, in winter, snow etches the outline of naked branches silhouetted against the sky, while a few bright berries still cling to the vines. Longview Farm is a perpetual joy.

*Summer is lush at Longview Farm and studded with a
superfluity of greens.*

*Autumn's harvest is gathered close to the pantry door while
houseplants stand nearby.*

When Joanna brings friends through her gardens, she loves to describe the scene as it was two months ago. A far-off look will creep into her eyes as she depicts the season just past. An expectant smile will play on her lips as she draws a profile of the season yet to come. And, all the while, the glory of those currently on display punctuates every step; it rushes with country exuberance around every bend.

Longview Farm did not begin life as a four-season garden. Joanna and and her fiancé George got the farm for a song in 1940 at a sheriff's sale. But, upon closer examination, the two began wondering if they had really bought a bargain—the house had extensive fire damage, the fields had not been farmed for decades, and the barn was precariously unstable. Nonetheless, they made plans to move in immediately after they were married.

The Reeds took a wedding trip touring historic gardens in Virginia and returned to their farm filled with hopes and dreams. But the newlyweds were rudely awakened from the first evening's sleep in the stucco cottage by a terrible stench wafting through an open window. Some hurried investigations quickly revealed the source of the effluvium: it was escaping from a manure pile delivered as a joint wedding present from both their fathers. As soon as the sun rose, they set to work spreading the potent gift far from their bedroom window—and so the garden was born.

Every week thereafter a list came from George's father with chores to be accomplished without delay. With the combined help and wisdom of their families and kindly neighbors, the farm fell into order. Livestock, seeds, and knowledge came as gifts from friends. Forever modest, Joanna will say, "There is not an original thought in my mind. Everything is

One of the Panoramic Vistas at Joanna Reed's Longview Farm

Although the country garden looks delightfully impulsive, Joanna admits, "I want it to look as if it just happened, but I need some underlying structure for my soul."

Among the first to poke buds above the snow-blanketed garden is the winter aconite (Eranthis hyemalis).

After a few spring showers, bleeding hearts (Dicentra spectabilis) *stretch their long chains of teardrop blossoms.*

borrowed from someone else." And yet, there is so much of Joanna in Longview Farm.

Before she married, Joanna was an art student. And from the very beginning, she yearned for beauty beyond the simple utility of the farm. Then one day, by chance, Dr. Albert Barnes of the Barnes

Foundation and Arboretum rang the front yard bell, his automobile stranded in front of the farmhouse. Before leaving in his repaired auto, Dr. Barnes invited Joanna to study at the arboretum. Of course, she eagerly accepted.

At the Barnes Foundation, Joanna learned propagation techniques as well as soil engineering and landscape design. Her studies changed the face of the land. "Frugality gives the garden continuity," Joanna observes while contemplating propagated shrubs wedged beside farmsheds and slipped amongst the fields. Somehow, although Joanna was busy raising five children, she always found time to plant, weed, and maintain her gardens. She always had a moment to welcome gardening friends.

It seems as though the laughter of house guests is forever filtering through the farmhouse's open windows. Joanna likes to say, "I love plants. But the people involved with gardening really drew me in— all gardeners are generous." For Joanna, part of the perpetual joy of gardening is the satisfaction of sharing. Whenever friends arrive, they find gardens filled with treasures; they leave with arms laden with bouquets of spring daffodils or baskets of freshly harvested summer squash. The gardens at Longview Farm give bountifully through all seasons of the year.

In spring, the gardens spill with generosity. Suddenly snow-blanketed fields burst into a patchwork of pastels. Shrubs that were naked only weeks before are bright and bushy with blossoms. The essence of the country is unabashed.

Spring is a heady season at Longview Farm. Fields of new flowers are sweet with the smell of April rains mingled delightfully with those spring bulbs and apple blossoms. Everywhere there is the glow of youth as hundreds of freshly born hues form

Blossoming dogwoods are scattered on the hill overlooking the old bootlegger's garage nestled not far from Joanna's barn.

a tapestry along fence rows. The country is particularly luscious in spring.

The bulbs are the first to shake off the snow. Grape hyacinths, snowdrops, crocus, scillas, and daffodils all poke buds from crystal patches of ice. Bulbs drift throughout the gardens. They wander down the fields, they nestle beside the farm house, and they dominate the banking in front of the red-trimmed barn. A frenzy of daffodils rushes down the entry drive, announcing spring's arrival to all passersby. Rounding the bend from the country road, narcissus and trillium combine with perennial powder-blue phlox and golden spurge (*Euphorbia epithymoides*) to extend a warm country welcome. Rare bulbs are sprinkled in—guinea hen fritillarias (*Fritillaria meleagris*) and cyclamen species. Joanna plants every bulb she can find, with the exception of tulips, which prove too much of a temptation for the pesky voles that torment her beds. "Tulips are caviar for the swine," she sighs.

Meanwhile, the long border that escorts the informal post-and-rail fence is awakening. Already, *Viola labradorica* is sending heart-shaped purple leaves wandering widely and wantonly. Primroses bristle with pert yellow blossoms, and wild columbines (*Aquilegia canadensis*) peek here and there, making surprise appearances from chance seedlings sown shamelessly everywhere. "That is how my garden grows," Joanna readily admits, "by chance."

Shocking golden winter aconite (*Eranthis hyemalis*) is among the first to greet the brave new season; a nosegay of sun-ray colored buds bursts from the snow surrounded by a bright green ruff of leaves. To complement the color, clusters of plump bluebells (*Hyacinthoides hispanica*) are scattered around, with magenta *Lunaria annua* sprinkled in

A statue which Joanna named Christopher resides in the patio garden in front of the farm house. Wax begonias and Begonia grandis *encircle his base.*

"for punch." Later in spring, mock oranges (*Philadelphus coronarius*) and French lilacs heighten the composition, adding puffs of color while infusing the air with intoxicating aroma.

If abundance is the essence of spring, then Joanna's garden is the epitome of the season. Every bed is richly clothed. Even in the woods, delightful wildlings such as bleeding hearts, epimedium, and ajuga don spring frocks. Beds of pink Lenten rose (*Helleborus orientalis*) and chartreuse *Helleborus foetidus* overlap seasons in March and April, singing together in a way that a sprinkling of blooms could never achieve. Fiddleheads unfold and creeping vinca scatters the floor with a firmament of blue

A path wanders out to the woodland from Joanna's back porch. In midsummer, it is edged with lemon yellow daylilies and spires of the false spirea (Sorbaria sorbifolia).

and white stars. Oceans of sweet woodruff (*Galium odoratum*) open their wine-sweet blossoms in May to cover the woodland floor with lace. Every footfall excites their perfume.

In summer, the land spills with bounty. Colors are bold and brazen, scents are rich and heady. If spring crept in with shy leaps and starts, summer is shameless. The bulbs that sang their delicate note in spring are replaced by a chorus in summer. Quiet pastels are upstaged by summer's vibrant primary shades in daring color compositions. The beds are ablaze with shimmering, sun-drenched hues.

The herb garden behind the farm house comes to life in summer's languid days. Originally, it began life as a boxwood parterre. As a surprise, Joanna levelled the five-foot slope behind the house while George was away on a business trip and then filled the terrace with soil bartered from a nearby railroad excavation. Boxwoods were planted in prim orderliness around a central urn. The formal scheme was very impressive, but the garden was doomed to failure. Voles tunneled in the loose soil, wreaking havoc with the boxwoods. After several shrubs had perished, Joanna decided to redesign the garden. Now, the backyard is instilled with the relaxed, simple splendor of a country herb garden.

For a birthday gift, Joanna's children rebedded the garden, adding three inches of gravel underneath and topping it off with fresh soil. They cut slate walkways to traverse rectangular beds surrounding the central urn. Then Joanna filled the beds with scented geraniums to spice the air with their delicious aromas; she laid out artemisias, campanulas, and yarrows to spread rough and tumble in their quadrants. In midsummer, the Mediterranean herbs sparkle in the blazing Pennsylvania sunshine

and send an exotic perfume up to the porch above. Salvias blossom in rainbow shades, rosemarys spill from beds, and silver lamb's ears (*Stachys byzantina*) drift between gray slate walkways.

Summer is a season of long days and sweltering sun at Longview Farm. Joanna awakens at dawn to begin her garden chores, often accomplishing three hours of work before breakfast. By noon, she can comfortably enjoy her gardens from the shade of the back porch overlooking the herb garden. From there, all the garden is a stage that Joanna can watch while sipping lemonade behind a screen of grapevines. Deer occasionally graze on the sweeping back lawn, hummingbirds visit fuchsias dangling from hanging baskets, and thieving birds steal grapes just an arm's length away. The summer slowly slips by.

Other gardens take up summer's lazy tempo. On the walled patio surrounding the front door of the farmhouse, boisterous pink wax begonias hug the border beside rosy sprays of the hardy tuberous begonia, *Begonia grandis*. Not far away, equally eye-catching cherry-red ivy geraniums nestle between felted silver dusty miller. Arbors of wisteria grow leafy and descend over the front door while a battalion of gathering baskets, spades, and straw hats hang close at hand, ready for a morning's work, serenaded by the drone of cicadas.

Daylilies stud the gardens with their fleeting but deliciously edible flowers.

Longview Farm in the Fall

Astilbe taquitta *'Superba' fills a field with colorful stands.*

By late summer, the meadows stretching beyond the barn are clothed in their most lavish colors. Behind the barn, Joanna's first garden overlooks a grassy hillside studded with wildflowers. Opulent perennial borders form a patina of color above and below a retaining wall that Joanna built herself. In fact, Joanna personally laid most of the stone walls that hem the farm, carefully keeping the soil level an inch or two higher than the top of retaining walls to prevent warping. And, of course, each wall is fitted with a series of drainage spouts to relieve the outpour of summer cloudbursts.

The first garden is bedded with low, crouching perennials that frame the meadow flowing up the hill. And, with quiet artistry, an upper board of the split-rail fence is discretely removed to reveal the farther wildflower meadow and its gazebo. The gazebo is another gift from Joanna's children. Given a choice of any style gazebo she wished, Joanna asked her children to refurbish a corn crib to flow with the mood of the place. Painted berry red to match the barn and positioned where the trees step aside to reveal the expansive vista of the Blue Hills in the distance, the summerhouse reigns over its meadow of black-eyed Susans, goldenrod, poverty grass, and daisies.

Joanna sweeps the meadow with her mower twice a year—in midsummer and early winter. To keep the meadow wildlings from encroaching on her beds, she cuts a swathe around the circumference of the field every two weeks. The grassy lawn behind the house is mowed at least once weekly, and the paths down from the hillside are also visited frequently by her mower. Joanna often clocks eighteen

Summer is a profusion of immodest colors as yarrows, phlox, and coneflowers glisten in the sun.

miles walking behind her rotary mower in a series of summer afternoons. But she loves every step along the way. "While mowing, I see vistas and discover little wonders that might otherwise slip by overlooked."

In autumn, the harvest begins. Wicker baskets and trugs are taken into the garden daily to return filled with cut yarrow, artemisia, and grasses for drying. Watering pots wait ready to receive the garden's last roses. And slowly, the garden dons a new set of clothes. Joanna's beds never look weary; they are carefully composed to prolong the growing season into the frosty dusk of the year. Around a deep cistern filled with waterlilies, *Sedum* 'Autumn Joy' transforms its flower heads from pink to burnished golden. Along the fence row border, *Hemerocallis* 'September Gold' holds huge amber

blossoms like torches beside the path. The flat umbels of the hardy ageratum (*Eupatorium coelestinum*) are scattered here and there, clustering in a purple blur wherever they happen to roam. White peas, *Lespedeza japonica*, sit not far from frilly late asters tumbling willy-nilly down the hillside.

The woodland gardens are on fire in autumn. Tall and proud, they border the open lawn behind the farmhouse, inundating in gentle waves of color. Tulip poplars (*Liriodendron tulipifera*) are the mainstay of the woods, turning a wondrous sulfur yellow in fall. Playing counterpoint, the sweet gums (*Liquidambar styraciflua*) flush to sparkling burgundy. Below, Japanese spirea (*Spiraea japonica* 'Gold Flame') bows and bends its vermillion branches in autumn gusts. *Viburnum dentatum* turns a subtle mauve, and a nearby *Viburnum dilatatum* is trans-

Autumn transforms Longview Farm with a new repertoire of shades; asters and black-eyed Susans lean on the split-rail fence.

formed into fiery shades amidst clusters of juicy red fruit. Long after the final sharp frost, berries still cling in Joanna's woods.

In winter, Joanna's garden holds that berry-red note, still overflowing with abundance. From the farmhouse, she can still watch birds chatter as they flit between naked branches, stealing fruit from the tangle of snow accented twigs. Icicles glisten from the split-rail fence as the garden's strongest features stand bared.

In midwinter, the harmony behind the melody at Longview Farm shines through. Suddenly, evergreens that slipped into the background in other seasons stand out tall and lacy. Beside the fence row, a statuesque Japanese cedar (*Cryptomeria japonica*) leans an elbow beside a majestic blue Atlas cedar (*Cedrus atlantica glauca*). Along the front drive, a topiary bunny skillfully carved of dwarf English yew (*Taxus cuspidata* 'Nana') whim-

sically hops through a pristine snow-white world.

Longview Farm seems warm in winter. Pasture gates, once whitewashed and now rubbed smooth by the hands of many visitors, stand invitingly unlatched and sprung open. Throughout the country fields, naked flower heads wave starkly against fields of snow. Strange seedpods from Joanna's rarities stand tall and stark, remnants from warmer days hinting of the garden's treasures.

Meanwhile, Joanna enjoys her garden from beside the fireplace in her home. There, in a shaft of winter sun, she sits on a window seat with an embroidery hoop slanting by her side. A bouquet of seedpods and dried flower heads sits on the table, and Joanna leans forward lost in thought. Slowly, carefully, she chooses a strand of embroidery wool, holds it to her bouquet to test the match and carefully threads her needle. Her eyes glisten with dreams and plans for next year's country garden.

Before the first frost, armloads of zinnias are cut for fleeting indoor bouquets. Yarrows and love-in-a-mist are bunched and hung from the rafters to dry.

Crewelwork Portraits of Her Garden

For a few brief moments in the morning, a shaft of sunlight streams through Joanna Reed's parlor windows. It plays lightly on a voluptuous bouquet waiting by the long wooden sideboard, and it illuminates the cards of embroidery wool that Joanna holds up to compare shades with the colors of the cut flowers.

Mornings may be hectic at Longview Farm, but Joanna always finds a minute to hold her crewel wool beside a blossom and match the colors by the early sunlight. "You can trust the first rays of the morning," she murmurs while jotting a color number beside a notebook sketch. Later in the evening or on a chilly winter afternoon, she can be found next to the window, bent over her embroidery frame, patiently stitching, with a huge basket of carded wool by her side. As Joanna stitches, flowers begin to take shape on the linen in her lap. She pulls the needle delicately in and out, recording a diary of her garden, chronicling the treasures of a season.

Spring's panel sets the pink foliage and blushing leaves of peach blossoms beside lilac blooms crafted in the lazy daisy stitch.

On spring's panel, primroses, trailing arbutus, and cucumber root sprout from pebbles worked in French knots.

Just as Joanna gardens with only well-crafted tools, she also

Grape hyacinths worked in French knots sit beside Solomon's seal, violets, and shortia.

seeks the very best sewing notions available. The fabric held taut in her embroidery frame is the finest Belgian twill. The warp is woven of linen for strength; the weft is cotton to lend softness to the fabric. It is a canvas that discriminating embroiderers have employed since the 1600s. She uses only Appleton wool, chosen for its subtle Old World colors and the spectrum of shades available. Her cards offer as many as eight values of each shade, allowing Joanna to compose her blossoms with all the subtlety of nature. Even more importantly, the wool is only one ply thick. The fine thread flatters Joanna's dexterous hand.

As Joanna works, she borrows her inspiration directly from nature. When the subject is lilacs, she keeps a bouquet of those fragrant blossoms close at hand so that she can scrutinize the shading in the floral spire by the early morning light. At her side, a vase holds a few open blossoms tucked beside a budded umbel and a withered spray so she can study the softest changes in the color and stature of lilacs throughout their brief lifetime. From her living models, Joanna sketches each blossom carefully onto a notepad with color notes penciled in the margins. Only a rough outline is etched on the fabric; the shading is improvised as she works. "A few dark stitches lend a third dimension," she explains if

asked how her yarrow succeeds in appearing so very lifelike.

Years ago, Joanna began studying embroidery, taking classes taught by experts. By 1970, she had gained sufficient confidence and expertise to begin a major project. Of course, that project had to incorporate her first love—botany. Joanna took wool and needle in hand to create a series of four curtains, each recording a season in her garden.

Originally, she planned to follow Jacobean traditions and embroider fanciful flowers to create a stylized garden on the cloth. But George, her husband, suggested that she apply her vast knowledge of horticulture to her artwork. So, instead of creating an imaginary garden, Joanna began stitching an astonishingly realistic diary of the blossoms growing around her. Twigs sprouted from the fabric, vines entwined the cloth, and flowers opened with incredible accuracy.

Two decades later, the finished curtains hang proudly on the west windows of the Reeds' cozy farmhouse. "Some of the flowers are gems; others are just stitches," Joanna says, perusing a resplendent panel of blossoms. Skunk cabbage, aconite, acorns, sumac, and snowdrops all bloom in a rich palette of subtle shades. Each delicate stitch is laid with intricate precision; colors are chosen with infinite care. Textures are laid by playing one stitch against the other. Stamens are crafted with tufted threads, pistils are fashioned from French knots, and shining fruit is created by weaving satin stitches close together. Leaves are composed of many subtle shades to hint at their veining and structure. Earth is given depth and scope by running waves of undulating chain stitches or weaving a latticework of varied threads. Some stitches are earnestly serious, others are lighthearted renderings—depending upon Joanna's mood. All her work is improvised; it evolves as her garden grows—by chance and whimsy.

Joanna began with winter, stitching the season's seeds, berries, and evergreens all sprouting from a single upwardly mobile trunk. It is a panel of subdued shades, of muffled mauves, burnished browns, and rich russets against a field of white linen. Amongst teal-colored holly leaves, satin-stitched berries shine. Elsewhere, olive Christmas ferns lay

On summer's panel, golden Clematis tangutica *and royal blue lupines interlace.*

flat against cross-stitched earth. Hundreds of tufted brown threads combine to create a chestnut burr, and sulfur chain stitches represent the winter-blooming petals of witch hazel. Through her fabric, Joanna discovered all the many-faceted hues of a hushed season.

Next, she stitched spring's bounty onto a curtain panel. Wending their way up a single trunk, peach-shaded rhododendron flowers touch a sprig of purple-budded *Ajuga reptans*. A dozen values of yellow combine to create glistening golden chain blossoms (*Laburnum anagyroides*) beside a peachy crown imperial flower. Collecting subjects amidst spring's frantic pace, Joanna found herself seeing individual blossoms for the

first time: "Now I note detail. I am intimate friends with flowers that were once just fleeting acquaintances."

Summer's panel was stitched while Joanna was away from her garden. While George was ill, the Reeds spent several summers sailing up the Hudson River and down the St. Lawrence. Everywhere she went, Joanna took her embroidery. "People knew me as the lady who went around dragging a large rag." And, along the way, she recorded a travel log, picking blossoms and stitching them into her curtains. She points to a *Clematis tangutica* outlined in buttonhole stitches and remembers a morning in Maine; she looks at a lupine and describes a summer afternoon in

Spring and summer scenes such as these, above and below, provide Joanna's inspiration for her crewelwork portraits.

the Gaspé Peninsula. Of course, Joanna also incorporated her own garden treasures into the scene. Daylilies are crosshatched in yellows and salmons, while weedy burdocks suddenly look lovely when composed of neat woolen spider stitches.

Autumn's fruit was recorded on the last panel, completed when Joanna was nearing her seventieth year. "I worried about this panel," Joanna admits. "I feared that my stitches would be uneven and the craftsmanship would not compare. Finally, I threw caution to the wind and just started stitching—and it seems the panel turned out to be as good as all the others."

With autumn, she worked with daring combinations of different shades. Muted peach and pink combine to represent the glowing hues that autumnal foliage turns before it fades. Thatched rose-hips, spider-stitched sunflowers, and buttonhole-stitched night-shades scramble up the single "tree of life" trunk. Each piece is worked with uncanny precision; each flower is crafted with incredible insight. Lustrous, glowing, and filled with a world of revelations, both Joanna and her garden are still growing.

BIOGRAPHIES

Blithewold Gardens and Arboretum

The VanWickle Family. Augustus Stout VanWickle, a coal baron, bought Blithewold in 1895 merely as a mooring for his newly acquired yacht. But gradually, he began to turn his interest from nautical pursuits toward improving the 33-acre property. John DeWolf, overseer for the design of Prospect Park in Brooklyn, New York, was commissioned to improve the grounds surrounding the summer mansion and, with his expertise, the arboretum was born.

Augustus spent several blissful summers at Blithewold with his wife, Bessie, and their daughter, Marjorie, until he was killed in a hunting accident in 1898. In his absence, his widow continued to visit Blithewold; she became a moving force behind the improvement of the grounds. She married William McKee in 1901, and together, they collected rare native and exotic plants to grace the grounds around their summer home.

Bessie passed away at Blithewold in 1936 and William McKee survived her by ten years, leaving the care of the arboretum to Marjorie upon his death in 1946. Marjorie, who became Mrs. George Lyon, had long felt a deep affection for the arboretum. And her strong, vivacious personality was immediately felt throughout the grounds. She continued to draw the town into her life and home; she opened the arboretum to the public every Fourth of July until her death at age 93 in 1976. To ensure that the arboretum would continue to flourish, she had arranged for the Heritage Foundation of Rhode Island to take over the preservation of Blithewold when she could no longer care for the grounds herself.

Dumbarton Oaks

Robert and Mildred Bliss. Just months after he graduated from Harvard University in 1900, Robert Bliss launched his diplomatic career, serving as private secretary to the governor of Puerto Rico. By 1903, he had joined the Foreign Service of the United States, serving in Venice, St. Petersburg, Brussels, and Buenos Aires. He was appointed as Minister to Sweden in 1923 and Ambassador to Argentina in 1927.

It was during Robert Bliss's Brussels appointment that he met Mildred Barnes. They were married in New York in 1908 and enjoyed a honeymoon en route to Buenos Aires. The couple had discovered many common interests immediately—their most fervent common bond was a love for collecting. Together, they focused their interests and amassed an incredible collection of Byzantine art and pre-Columbian artifacts.

In Autumn of 1919, the Blisses returned to Washington, and seized the moment to find a home for their ever-increasing collections. After a little searching, they found Dumbarton Oaks and summoned two close friends—Royall Tyler, a scholar who had guided their collections, and Beatrix Farrand, who had designed a garden for Mildred Bliss's mother—to survey the place. The landscape was well on its way toward transformation into a lush labyrinth of gardens by the time Robert Bliss was summoned to Sweden in 1923.

When they returned to Georgetown a decade later, their home attracted an elite crowd of scholars, artists, and musicians. In 1945, when asked about his hobbies, Robert Bliss replied, "My hobbies? My wife and Dumbarton Oaks!"

In the late 1930s, the Blisses began purchasing books on Byzantine and pre-Columbian art to create a library to complement their art collections. When the library was completed in 1940, Dumbarton Oaks was given to Harvard University to become a living museum open to expansion and change. Robert Bliss died in 1962 and Mildred Bliss passed away seven years later. Their ashes are buried in the wall overlooking their resplendent rose garden.

Beatrix Farrand. Dumbarton Oaks is a story of a friendship as well as the tale of a landscape molded into a small piece of paradise preserved. It is the saga of a liaison between Mildred Bliss and Beatrix Farrand, the landscape artist.

Born in New York City in 1872, Beatrix Jones knew her father only 12 years when her parent's marriage was dissolved in divorce and her father departed for Paris. At the time, most divorced women wallowed miserably in disgrace, but not Mary Cadwalader Jones. Her drawing room became a popular meeting place for New York City's literati. Henry James frequently visited the house and Edith Wharton, her former husband's sister, remained so close that Mary Jones occasionally acted as a literary agent for Ms. Wharton's writing. Undoubtedly, that atmosphere influenced Beatrix's work.

Beatrix was pursuing an education when she met Mrs. Charles Sargent, the wife of the founder of the Arnold Arboretum. Soon she was studying botany at the arboretum, although no woman had dared to pursue such an avenue previously. In 1895, Beatrix traveled extensively throughout Europe, all the while learning from the landscapes that she visited.

Immediately upon returning from her travels, Beatrix opened an office in New York and began receiving commissions through her many social connections. Merely three years later, in 1899, she was invited to become a founding member of the American Society of Landscape Architects.

At the age of 41, Beatrix married Dr. Max Farrand, chairman of the Yale History Department, and went to live with him in San Marino, California, where she designed the home of Henry Huntington. Other important landscapes designed by Beatrix Farrand include the campus of the University of Chicago (1929–1936), Princeton University (1912–1943), Yale University (1922–1945), and the Abby Aldrich Rockefeller Garden at Seal Harbor, Maine (1926–1950).

Although Beatrix dearly loved Dumbarton Oaks, she was also devoted to Reef Point, her mother's property at Bar Harbor, Maine. When it became evident that she could not assure perpetual care for the landscape, she donated her library and herbarium to the University of California at Berkeley. Beatrix survived her husband by 14 years, living at Bar Harbor until her death in 1959.

The Emily Dickinson Homestead

Emily Dickinson. Most of the secrets of Emily Dickinson's solitary life remain as enigmatic as her cryptic poems. She was born in December of 1830 in Amherst, Massachusetts, and grew up in a house near the center of town, built by her grandfather. She spent all but 15 years of her life in that home. Her generous grandfather found himself bankrupt in 1840, and was forced to sell the family house. Emily's father, Edward, a successful lawyer and politician, purchased another house beside the cemetery in Amherst and the family settled there until they could buy their home again in 1855.

Emily lived a rather ordinary life in her youth—she was, from all accounts, a very social young lady and enrolled in Mount Holyoke Female Seminary, where she studied for a year before returning home.

Emily was a petite woman with a fervent heart and an intensity that bubbled from her heart. In 1862, Emily sent a packet of her poems to a family friend, Thomas Wentworth Higginson, asking if they "breathed." He encouraged her, so she continued to write poetry in every spare moment that could be stolen. During her lifetime, only seven of her poems were published, and those anonymously. Most of her writing was scribbled on slips of paper and tucked away. Her talent remained a lifelong secret, even from those closest to her.

As the years wore on, Emily drew her family and a few close friends around her. She delighted in their company, and she immersed herself in the garden, orchard, fields, and meadows that surrounded her home. And she wrote wonderful insights about the animals, blossoms, and other creatures that populated her world. After 1855, Emily focused her life totally around the Dickinson Homestead, leaving her father's house only twice in the 31 years before her death in 1886.

The week following Emily's death, her sister found what scholars estimate as 1800 of Emily's poems and packets of personal letters, all carefully tied with ribbons and stored in a drawer. For reasons that the world will probably never know, Lavinia burned most of the correspondence and all but 700 of the poems. What remained was later published, establishing Emily Dickinson as one of this country's greatest poets.

The Will C. Curtis Garden in the Woods

Will C. Curtis and Howard "Dick" Stiles. Will C. Curtis was a full-time nursery manager and a part-time landscape designer when he happened upon the 30-acre plot in Framingham, Massachusetts, that would become his Garden in the Woods. He had been searching for such a

place since childhood. He later wrote, "Grandfather was a civil engineer by profession but a farmer by choice, a man who loved the land, observed what grew upon it, and appreciated its beauty. I was his shadow. Before I could read, he had taught me how to spell many words, chiefly those describing trees, plants, and the earth's terrain."

Will purchased the land and began planting the landscape of his dreams. He worked easily with nature, but did not interact as smoothly with people. The upkeep of the expansive wildflower garden required the expertise of a full-time caretaker, and a series of gardeners came and went until Howard "Dick" Stiles arrived on the scene. Dick was in his mid-twenties, unemployed, and penniless—this was the Depression. Initially, the young man knew nothing of gardening, but he was eager to work and so gradually learned the ways of the woods. Eventually, the two became partners, designing and filling the garden with a forest of native shrubs and foreign rarities.

When old age limited Will's landscape-design income, the two looked for someone to shoulder responsibility for the garden's upkeep. In 1965 the New England Wild Flower Society established its headquarters on the grounds. Will Curtis died four years later at the age of 86, content in the knowledge that he had created a lasting legacy. Dick Stiles retired from the garden in 1970 and passed away in 1984 at the age of 74.

The Gardens at Cranbrook House

George Booth. Born in Toronto, Canada, in 1864, George Gough Booth grew up surrounded by the crisp beauty of the north country. One of ten children, George's formal education ceased at the age of 14, and yet he continued to study independently. When his family moved to Detroit, George dabbled in architectural design and ornamental ironwork, honing a sophisticated taste for art that would later blossom at Cranbrook.

Although George's career began in the arts, it took an abrupt turn in 1887 when he married Ellen Scripps, daughter of James E. Scripps, owner of the *Detroit Evening News*. A year later, George was the newspaper's business manager; soon after he was buying and selling small papers at a profit. In 1914 George and his brother, Ralph Harmon Booth, founded the Booth Newspapers, Inc., which grew to become the largest newspaper chain in Michigan.

Whenever he could escape from the city, George took a spin in his automobile, bouncing down the rough and dusty roads of the countryside with Ellen and their five children in the back seat. George found the land in Bloomfield Hills so alluring that in 1905 he purchased a 325-acre tract. He hired Albert Kahn, a well-known architect, to design a splendid red brick mansion at the crest of a hill.

The Booths were active patrons of the Arts and Crafts Movement in America. For several years, George harbored a dream of building an art school community. When he met Eliel Saarinen, a Finnish architect who was teaching at the University of Michigan in 1924, the two began laying plans for his community. Saarinen designed the wonderful buildings that grace the grounds.

Ellen Scripps Booth died in 1948 and George passed away the following year. In their absence, the school grounds have been faithfully maintained, but the gardens were left untended until 1971 when the Booths' youngest son, Henry Scripps Booth, founded the Cranbrook House and Gardens Auxiliary. Devoted volunteers have restored the gardens to their former majesty.

Wing Haven

Elizabeth and Edwin Clarkson. Elizabeth Barnhill and Edwin Clarkson met in Boston; Elizabeth was studying at the New England Conservatory of Music, and Edwin, a young engineer with a degree from North Carolina State College, was working for a local textile company. When Elizabeth graduated and began touring the country as a concert pianist, Edwin followed her, appearing in the audience wherever she performed. Finally, she agreed to become his wife.

While the couple was engaged, Elizabeth returned home to Uvalde, Texas, and designed their future home in Charlotte, North Carolina, and Edwin set to work building the house. When it was finished, he drove out to Texas to marry his bride. Having driven from Texas to Charlotte, the honeymooners arrived at their new home on an April evening in 1927. Elizabeth's dreams were shattered on the spot. The house sat in the midst of a barren field; pathetically poor clay soil stretched as far as her eye could see. The very next morning, she set to work planting the garden that would become Wing Haven.

For a wedding gift, Edwin gave his new bride a Steinway baby grand piano so she would not feel lonesome for the music she loved. But, as her gardens grew, Elizabeth practiced piano less often and eventually let that part of her life go entirely to devote her full attention to birds and botany. She gave programs on wildlife gardening to school children and wrote a guide to attracting birds entitled *Birds of Charlotte and Mecklenburg County, North Carolina* in 1944. In the Clarkson's living room, a chapter of the Audubon Society was formed in 1940.

A gentle, soft-spoken, but also strong-willed woman, Elizabeth had a natural affinity with animals. When she passed away in 1988, Wing Haven's future was secure under the auspices of Wing Haven Foundation, a non-profit organization formed in 1970. Edwin Clarkson is now 91 and lives nearby. He visits the bird sanctuary frequently.

Longwood Gardens

Pierre S. du Pont. Born in 1870 in Christiana Hundred, Delaware, Pierre S. du Pont was the eldest of eleven children. Pierre grew up in a family that had already made its mark on the industrial world—young Pierre was the great-grandson of Eleuthère Irénée du Pont who came to this country from France in 1800 and founded the Du Pont chemical company.

Pierre's father had broken away from the family business to form his own chemical company when, in 1884, he was killed in a factory explosion leaving the 14-year-old Pierre as head of the family. Pierre continued with his education, eventually graduating from the Massachusetts Institute of Technology. He joined Du Pont Chemical Company and eventually became president. Later he would run General Motors, and rescue it from bankruptcy.

Pierre was 36 years and still unmarried when he purchased Peirce's Park, a 250-acre arboretum in Kennett Square, Pennsylvania. He immediately set to work improving the grounds and, by 1909, Pierre was entertaining friends at his new home.

At first, Pierre hired a landscape architect to inventory the trees in his arboretum and offer suggestions for improvement. Disappointed with the proposal set forth by the professionals, Pierre designed Longwood himself—and with incredible ability. All of his artistic, engineering, and horticultural talents came to play as he molded the estate into a masterpiece. In 1919, he added a crowning element—he began construction of an immense conservatory, which opened in 1921.

In 1915 Pierre married his cousin, Alice Belin from Scranton, Pennsylvania, who shared his affection for horticulture. They traveled together through Italy and France seeking ideas for the estate. Alice died in 1944 and Pierre succeeded her by ten years. Upon his death, he left Longwood Gardens "for the sole use of the public for purposes of exhibition, instruction, education, and enjoyment."

The Huntington Botanical Gardens

Henry Huntington. Born in 1850 in Oneonta, New York, Henry Edwards Huntington moved to California in 1892 to manage the Southern Pacific Railroad for his uncle Collis Potter Huntington. He purchased a 600-acre ranch in San Marino, ten miles northeast of the city, to which he commuted frequently. He quickly realized the potential of public transportation, and after selling the railroad he devoted his attention to developing the Pacific Electric line, the largest inter-urban system of its day.

Henry Huntington had other interests—by 1907 he began vigorously collecting art, sharing his passion for masterpieces with Arabella Huntington, Uncle Collis's widow. Concentrating on British art of the Georgian period and French eighteenth-century decorative art, they began to amass an impressive collection. In 1913, Henry and Arabella were married and moved into a newly finished Beaux Arts mansion that Henry had built on his ranch.

After Henry's retirement from the railroad in 1908, he began improving his landscape. At first, his tastes took a commercial bent. In 1911 he created the first commercial avocado grove and also experimented to create new varieties of citrus, apricots, peaches, persimmons, sapotes, and jujubes. But, as his interest in the beauty of art grew, he began to search for rare plants.

The Huntington collections were always open to scholars. In 1919, Henry founded the Huntington Institute to ensure that the public would always have access to his collection. Arabella passed away in 1924 and Henry died in 1927. Both are buried in a neo-classic mausoleum overlooking the Huntington Botanical Gardens.

Celia Thaxter's Island Garden

Celia Thaxter. In 1939, when Celia Laighton was only four years old, she left the mainland and traveled with her family to their new home on White Island, one of the Isles of Shoals ten miles off the coast of Portsmouth, New Hampshire. On that sparse, rocky land, her father became the lighthouse keeper.

Eight years later, Celia's father built Appledore House, a summer resort on Appledore, the largest of the Isles of Shoals. And so Celia's contact with the outside world began. A dashing Harvard student, Levi Thaxter, was engaged as a tutor, and it was not long before he requested Celia's hand.

Celia left Appledore to live on the mainland, where she grew deeply homesick for the ocean. In the midst of one long winter, she wrote her first poem entitled "Landlocked." A friend secretly forwarded it to *The Atlantic*

Monthly, where it appeared in 1860, launching Celia's career as a poet.

Meanwhile, Celia returned to Appledore every summer to help at the hotel and to garden around the cottage where her parents had once lived. She and her literary friends spent long hours immersed in discussion amid the sparkling poppies in her garden.

Celia Thaxter died in 1894, ten years after her husband passed away, and she was buried on Appledore. Her books included *Poems* (1872) and *Among the Isles of Shoals* (1873). But Celia Thaxter's affection for gardening is revealed vividly in the pages of *An Island Garden*, published in 1894.

Joanna Reed's Longview Farm

Joanna Reed. Born in West Virginia in 1917, Joanna McQuail traveled to Philadelphia every winter to attend school. "Back in those days, you could not get much of an education in West Virginia," she explains. She attended the Philadelphia Museum School of Industrial Arts (now the University of the Arts). She spent two years studying illustration, gaining a background in art.

In 1940, Joanna and her fiancé, George Reed, purchased a 49-acre tract of land in Chester County, Pennsylvania, at a sheriff's sale. They were married in April and, following a brief wedding trip touring Virginia gardens, the couple immediately set to work planting their first garden.

Originally, the Reeds hoped to make their living as farmers, but the road was fraught with perils. The magnificent 1780 barn, which had caught Joanna's eye when she first found the farm, partially collapsed the day the Reeds received the deed for the land. They gradually built their stock into an inventory that finally included 300 chickens, 50 summer turkeys, and assorted sheep, pigs, horses and a pony. Supplementing their farm income with George's earnings as an engineer, the Reeds raised their family of five children. Over the years, Joanna also incorporated her artistic skills into the grounds of Longview Farm, transforming the farm fields into lush and friendly landscapes.

In 1965, Joanna Reed became a member of the Herb Society of America and later hosted their annual plant sale in her voluminous country barn. She served as their national president from 1980 to 1982 and raised funds for the herb garden at the National Arboretum in Washington, D.C. In 1984, Joanna was awarded the Herb Society's Medal of Honor. In addition, her deft crewelwork has won numerous Embroiderers' Guild blue ribbons.

George Reed passed away in 1982 and Joanna continues to care for Longview Farm in his absence. In 1990, she held a splendid picnic, celebrating 50 years of gardening around her home.

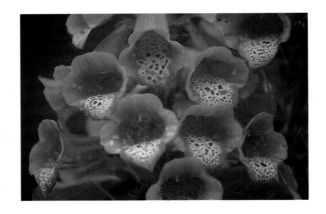

VISITOR'S INFORMATION

BLITHEWOLD GARDENS AND ARBORETUM
Ferry Road
Bristol, RI 02809
Phone: (401) 253-8714

Garden hours: January through December, 10:00 A.M. to 4:00 P.M.

CRANBROOK HOUSE AND GARDENS
380 Lone Pine Road
Bloomfield Hills, MI 48013
Phone: (313) 645-3147

Garden hours: May 1 through Memorial Day, Saturdays and Sundays only; Memorial Day through Labor Day, daily including holidays; Labor Day through October 31, Saturdays and Sundays only 1:00 P.M. to 5:00 P.M.

THE WILL C. CURTIS GARDEN IN THE WOODS
New England Wild Flower Society
Garden in the Woods
Hemenway Road
Framingham, MA 01701
Phone: (508) 877-6574

Garden hours: April 15 to October 31, Tuesday through Sunday 9:00 A.M. to 4:00 P.M.

EMILY DICKINSON HOMESTEAD
280 Main Street
Amherst, MA 01002
Phone: (413) 542-8161

Homestead hours: By appointment only, May through October 1:30 P.M. to 3:45 P.M. Wednesday through Saturday only. Closed from December 15 to March 1.

DUMBARTON OAKS
1703 32nd Street NW
Washington, DC 20007
Phone: (202) 338-8278

*Garden hours: April through October,
2:00 P.M. to 6:00 P.M. daily. November
through March, 2:00 P.M. to 5:00 P.M.
daily. Closed on national holidays and
during inclement weather.*

HUNTINGTON BOTANICAL GARDENS
1151 Oxford Road
San Marino, CA 91108
Phone: (818) 405-2141

*Garden hours: Tuesday through Friday
1:00 P.M. to 4:30 P.M., Saturday and
Sunday 10:30 A.M. to 4:30 P.M. Closed
Monday and major holidays.*

LONGWOOD GARDENS
Route 1
Kennett Square, PA 19348
Phone: (215) 388-6741

*Garden hours: April through October,
9:00 A.M. to 6:00 P.M. daily. November
through March, 9:00 A.M. to 5:00 P.M.
daily. Conservatories: 10:00 A.M. to 5:00
P.M. daily.*

JOANNA REED'S LONGVIEW FARM
P.O. Box 766, RD #1
Malvern, PA 19355
Phone: (215) 827-7614

*Garden hours: April through October—
Friday, Saturday, and Sunday, noon to
dusk. Do not call, just stop by and ring
the bell.*

CELIA THAXTER'S ISLAND GARDEN
Appledore is accessible only by taking a
ferry from Portsmouth, New Hampshire.
For ferry schedules contact:
The Shoals Marine Laboratory
G 14 Stimson Hall
Cornell University
Ithaca, NY 14853
Phone: (607) 255-3717

WASHINGTON NATIONAL
CATHEDRAL
Massachusetts and Wisconsin
Avenues, NW
Washington, DC 20016-5098
Phone: (202) 537-6200

Garden hours: Sunrise to 7:00 P.M. daily.

WING HAVEN
Wing Haven Foundation
248 Ridgewood Avenue
Charlotte, NC 28209
Phone: (704) 331-0664 or 332-5770

*Garden hours: Sunday 2:00 to 5:00 P.M.
and Tuesday and Wednesday 3:00 to 5:00
P.M. throughout the year*

AFTERWORD

When I photograph gardens, flowers, and all the scenery of nature, I always think that I will never be able to portray the same sight the same way again. Even if the same flower were to bloom next spring in the same place, neither the subtle patterns of light nor the invisible currents in the air that nature creates can ever occur again. Never resisting nature, by watching the delicate light that continually changes and the flowers and leaves of trees that every minute, every second change their appearance, I work to blend my emotions and sensibilities with flowers, trees, and their surroundings through the camera lens.

One of the reasons I never tire of photographing New York City's Central Park, which I have photographed for so many years, is because the beauty of nature changes every day. There are always new discoveries each time a place, photographed previously, is revisited.

Frequently, the first time I visit a garden, partic-

ularly when there is a time limitation, I become so absorbed in the work that I forget even to eat. Ideally, I should be able to photograph within just one day, from dawn to dusk, the sight of a garden enveloped in morning haze, the boughs and leaves wet with rain, the soft sunlight or the powerful rays of the sun that break through the clouds after a rainfall, and the spectacle that all of these join to create, the mystical appearance of the flowers that bloom in the deepening summer dusk, or the garden blanketed in the pure, cool white snow of winter— the list is endless.

Whether private or public, large or small, each garden, like each flower or each person, has its own beautiful individuality. Having visited many gardens, I was happiest about having met so many wonderful people who loved flowers and nature. I would like to express my deep gratitude to the many gardeners, the people who helped with the photography, and to the editors of *Victoria*.

Toshi Otsuki, Photographer
New York City
Early Spring, 1991

ACKNOWLEDGMENTS

This book could not have been created without the generosity of so many gardeners. We are greatly indebted to the friends who helped us to see and understand their gardens.

In particular we would like to thank Mark Zelonis and Julie Morris of Blithewold; Diane Kostial McGuire and Eleanor M. McPeck, historians of Dumbarton Oaks and Beatrix Farrand; Miss Parke at the Dickinson Homestead; Barbara Pryor and David Giblin at Garden in the Woods; Kathleen Sheean, Mary Ann Krear, Jane Clark, Roz Basherian, and the Auxiliary at Cranbrook Gardens; Mrs. Guy Steuart III, Maureen Elonzo, Polly Mitchell, and the All Hallows Guild at Washington Cathedral; Wanny Hogewood at Wing Haven; Robert Herald,

Colvin Randall, and William H. Frederick, Jr., at Longwood Gardens; Leslie Land for creating a wonderful white garden; Deborah Queen of Anna Caplan for her antique Wardian Case; Claire Martin, Shirley Kerins, Ann Richardson, and Lisa Blackburn of the Huntington Botanical Gardens; Chris Bobdanovick at Celia Thaxter's Island Garden; Sharon Ackland of La Petite Fleur for her artistic and aromatic potpourris; and Joanna Reed and her entire family for their warm hospitality.

Our gratitude, as well, to the staff of *Victoria* for their cooperation in making this book possible. To Charles Glaser, photography editor, in particular, who makes it a joy to review the thousands of transparencies we selected from for *Moments in the Garden*.

In the spring, color rules the day at Joanna Reed's Longview Farm.

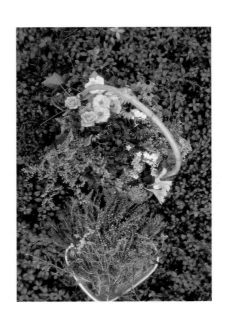